CATEGORY IS: Cocktails!

David Dodge and David Orton
Illustrated by Cheyne Gallarde

CATEGORY IS:

Cocktails!

Mixed Drinks
Inspired by
Legendary Drag
Performers

Prestel

Munich · London · New York

Contents

Introduction

Cocktails and drag shows go together hand in hand—like heckling at a Bianca Del Rio performance. It's a real wig-scratcher, then, that there has never been a cocktail book devoted exclusively to the Drag High Arts. Fortunately, those dark days are finally over: in these hallowed pages, you will read about some of the world's most legendary drag stars and learn to make cocktails and zero-proof drinks inspired by their storied lives and careers.

Having a cocktail created in your image is obviously the highest honor any human can receive, and some may question whether drag artists are worthy of such prestige. To these doubters we say, read on: in this book, you will learn about sixty performers who are *also* celebrated makeup artists, dancers, and actors. You will be awed by comedians, costume designers, community activists, and contortionists. You will toast Emmy winners, Broadway stars, and astronauts.

Okay, we have—yet!—to send a drag queen to space (when we do, hopefully Lady Bunny is available), but you get the point: drag performers are true artists. They excel in a dizzying number of fields while also helping us examine, question, and laugh at the gender norms that lead to so much misogyny, queerphobia, and transphobia—a development so threatening to some that they are literally trying to ban the art form. That a drag performer can embody all this while simultaneously cracking a poop joke seems pretty worthy of an artisanal drink, don't you think? (Honestly, Neil Armstrong could never …)

If you've picked up this book, fellow drag lover, chances are we don't need to convince you of the art form's worthiness. Hopefully, you're even sympathetic to the difficulty we faced in narrowing down the performers included to just sixty. The weight of this responsibility was not lost on us—this book *will* make or break entire careers. But here's the Long-Island-Iced tea of it all: it would be an impossible task to perfectly represent drag's rich history within a single book. So we didn't even try! Instead, we present just a narrow sliver of its breadth and reach, which truly spans generations, genders, and geographies.

We picked some no-brainers, like global sensations Trixie Mattel and Pabllo Vittar. We also included people who paved the way for those performers' current superstardom, such as Divine, who ate literal dog shit in *Pink Flamingos* so that RuPaul could one day implore us to "work."

Speaking of Mama Ru, no book on drag could be complete without healthy representation from a little reality TV competition called *RuPaul's Drag Race*. Ours is no different, and rightfully so—the show has single-handedly mainstreamed drag, launched the careers of hundreds of queens, and inspired an entirely new generation of aspiring drag artists. It's unfortunate there has yet to be a platform of similar stature to celebrate the work of drag kings and nonbinary and genderqueer drag artists, who are just as plentiful and talented as their sisters. However, performers like Landon Cider, Sin Wai Kin, and Murray Hill are far too booked and busy to notice any lack of opportunity.

There are plenty of people in this book who have never graced the *Drag Race* main stage. These include historical figures like vaudevillian king Annie Hindle, whose drag fooled ministers into consecrating her same-sex marriage in the 1880s, and local queens like Elishaly D'witshes, known for jumping off double-decker buses on Miami's South Beach and landing in the splits. They may not be household names, but such iconic behavior *cannot* go untoasted.

Now, for a quick note on pronouns: in the eloquent words of Gottmik, "gender is stupid." Still, we have done our due diligence to use the preferred pronouns of each performer in this book. But, much like Jinkx Monsoon's sewing abilities, gender is elusive and amorphous—many artists change their preferred pronouns over time (Adore Delano once said her preferred pronoun was "pizza") or use different markers when in or out of drag. If this concept is simply too much, we have just the cocktail for you: the Old Fashioned! (Zing!)

It's a testament to drag's cultural impact and significance today that there are so many incredible artists worthy of a tribute drink. If your most beloved performer isn't included, we hope you take inspiration from this book and whip up your very own cocktail recipe to toast *your* fave! We implore you to consider this option before coming for us on Twitter, dear drag stans. We are very scared of you.

David Dodge and David Orton

Basic Equipment

A drag artist is nothing without their accessories—and the same goes for the at-home bartender. Here are some of the tools you'll need on hand to create the tribute cocktails in this book.

Shaker
Boston shaker? I hardly know her! Despite sounding like an old-timey drag club in Beantown, a Boston shaker is in fact a bartending tool for cocktail making, consisting of a large metal can and a slightly smaller mixing glass. A Cobbler shaker, meanwhile, has a built-in strainer and cap in addition to a metal mixing can—and is all you'll need unless you're fixing to become the world's next bartending superstar.

Strainer
A Hawthorne strainer is a flat, perforated metal disc with a coiled spring around the edge that looks like some kind of terrifying medical tool. Actually, it's just a device that fits over your shaker to strain your cocktail—you'll need one if you're using a Boston shaker. You can also use a fine mesh strainer to remove small chunks of ice, muddled fruits, or spices from your drink.

Jigger/shot glass
A jigger is someone who dances to Irish folk music—but it's also a shot glass used to measure alcohol and other liquid ingredients for cocktails. They come in different sizes. In this book, one shot measures 1 fl. oz., or 30 ml.

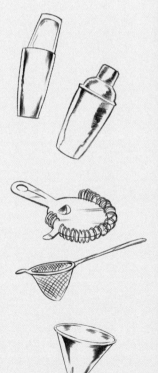

Citrus squeezer
If the juice wasn't worth the squeeze … you likely didn't have this helpful tool in your arsenal! A handheld citrus squeezer will aid you in extracting every last tasty drop from lemons, limes, and other citrus fruits.

Mixing glass
For cocktails that are stirred and not shaken, you can simply use your shaker, a pint glass, or a 7-Eleven Big Gulp cup for the task. But if you really want to impress friends with your bartending prowess, get a fancy mixing glass to stir your ingredients in, before straining them into a serving glass.

Bar spoon
A bar spoon is a long, thin spoon used to stir cocktails in a mixing glass or shaker; it can also measure small quantities of spirits. It has a twisted handle that makes it easier to spin between the fingers while stirring.

Muddler
A muddler is used to crush (or muddle) fruits, herbs, and spices in the bottom of a glass or shaker to release their flavors and aromas. Most have a long, sturdy handle and a bottom that's either flat or rounded. Muddlers can be made of wood or any other hard material. (Anyone else hot and bothered after reading that?)

Blender
Blenders are used to mix frozen or crushed ice drinks, as well as specific ingredients to help create an even texture and more consistent flavor.

Glassware

If a drag artist's canvas is the face, the bartender's is the glass. Make sure you have the following glassware on hand to properly beat the faces of the cocktails in this book.

Highball/Collins glass
Highball and Collins glasses are often confused for one another since they are both tall and slender, but a Collins is slightly taller and slenderer—a fact she just loves to lord over poor Highball. Either glass is perfect for making cocktails with a higher ratio of mixer to spirit.

Rocks glass
A rocks glass is the Jiggly Caliente of cocktail glasses: short, squat, and ready to be filled up with an assortment of mixed drinks—like an Old Fashioned, a Negroni, or a Manhattan. It typically has a thick base and is designed to hold ice and a small amount of alcohol, allowing the drinker to savor the flavors and aromas of the cocktail.

Martini/cocktail glass
A Martini (or cocktail) glass is a stemmed glass with a cone-shaped bowl that is typically used for drinks served straight up (without ice), like Martinis and Cosmopolitans. Pro tip: if your drink tastes like shit, you can always serve it to guests in a Martini glass to fool them into thinking it's fancy.

Nick and Nora glass
A Nick and Nora glass is stemmed with a rounded bowl that is similar to a Martini glass but with deeper sides and a bit smaller. It's named after the fictional detectives from the 1930s *Thin Man* film series. Like a Martini or coupe glass, the Nick and Nora is great for any drink served straight up. It also has a narrower rim, making it the perfect choice for your spill-prone guests. Think of it as the sippy cup of cocktail glasses.

Coupe

A coupe is a stemmed glass with a shallow, saucer-shaped bowl that is wider than a traditional Martini glass. This larger surface area allows the aromas to develop even more and makes it a bit less likely to spill. Even if you do, who cares? Everyone looks elegant with a coupe in hand!

Champagne flute

A champagne flute is the Violet Chachki of cocktail glasses—impossibly skinny, stems for days, and a small head that tapers slightly towards the top. It's designed to enhance the effervescence and aroma of champagne or sparkling wine by allowing the bubbles and tastes to rise to the surface, concentrating at the top of the glass.

Hurricane glass

A Hurricane glass is curvy and tall, with a flared rim and a narrow base. It's typically used for tropical, blended, or frozen drinks like Hurricanes or Margaritas. Perfect for your next tiki party, Cinco de Mayo fiesta, or any other cultural festivity you'd like to appropriate.

Wine glass

Wine glasses enhance flavors and aromas and are perfect for (see if you can guess ...) wine-based drinks like sangria and spritzers.

Shot glass

A shot glass, the preferred drinking vessel of college students and reality show contestants, can also be used to create small, elegant sipping cocktails served neat.

Mule mug

A Mule mug is made of copper and typically includes a handle for ease of use. Its name comes from the Moscow Mule—where the copper quickly absorbs the cold temperature of the drink, keeping it cool for longer.

Nontraditional glassware

Drag artists are anything but traditional, so toast your favorite queen or king in whatever random glassware you might have lying around the house! In this book, you'll see recipes calling for a soda fountain glass, a decorative goblet, a hollowed-out pineapple, a teacup, and more. This is drag, after all—channel your inner Trixie Mattel and color outside the contour lines!

Cocktail Ingredients

The drinks in this book call for everything from cocktail weenies to liquids meant to mimic various bodily fluids—which should give you some indication that in cocktail making, like drag, there really aren't very many rules about materials you can use for your finished product. Still, here are some of the basic ingredients you'll want to have on hand.

Alcohol

Much like drag artists, the personality profiles of alcohols run the gamut from super sweet to bitter as hell. The most common spirits to use as your base include gin, vodka, rum, tequila, whiskey, and brandy. Each has its own unique flavor and characteristics that make it the best choice for specific types of cocktails. Want a subtle taste that doesn't overpower your ingredients? Vodka will be the best Judy for the job. Looking for a smoky punch to the palette? A spirit like mezcal will do the trick. (For more detail on the booze called for in this book, check out the next section.)

Citrus and fruit juices

Citrus and fruit juices add natural sweetness, acidity, and refreshing flavors to cocktails. The most popular citrus juices used in cocktails are lemon, lime, and grapefruit, which help to balance out the sweetness of other ingredients. You'll often find recipes that call for fruit juices as well, like cranberry, pineapple, or orange, which add desired flavors and colors to a drink. Who doesn't love a good ombré effect? To ensure the best-tasting cocktail, squeeze those fruits fresh, sweetie!

Simple syrup/honey syrup

Bartenders use simple syrup to help sweeten up a drink. As
the name implies, it's very simple to make! Mix together one
cup (200 g) of sugar and one cup (240 ml) of water over low
heat, without letting the mixture come to a boil, and stir until
the sugar is completely dissolved. The resulting syrup is a clear
liquid with a honey-like consistency, which you can store in
your fridge for up to a month. In the above recipe you can
also replace the sugar with the same quantity of honey for
a variation with a more unique flavor profile.

Club soda and carbonated drinks

You can give your taste buds a refreshing little bubble bath
by adding a carbonated mixer to your cocktail. Some popular
examples include club soda (aka soda water), tonic water,
ginger ale, and cola, which can help create a well-balanced
and flavorful beverage. (They're also a convenient way to
water down drinks for your overserved friends.) As any
quick trip to the supermarket will reveal, the options here
are endless. However, dry, Italian-style sodas have less sugar
than traditional ones and can be a great way to add flavor and
effervescence without too much additional sweetness.

Bitters

Bitters are highly concentrated flavoring agents made by
infusing herbs, spices, fruits, nuts, and botanicals into alcohol.
The most famous of these is Angostura bitters, made from the
gentian root. Careful not to overdo it! A little bit goes a long way.

Eggs and foamers

You can use egg whites to add a frothy texture and subtle
richness to a drink, as well as to help balance out the acidity of
citrus ingredients. When shaken with other ingredients, egg
whites create a foam that sits on top of a cocktail, adding both
visual and textural appeal. For a vegan alternative, see pp. 20–21.

Infused alcohols

For the sake of ease and simplicity, we've mostly steered away
from using infused alcohols in this book. However, if you're
wanting to take your cocktail game to the next level, you can
make infused booze at home.

Types of Alcohol

Cocktails, like drag artists, are defined by their unique spirits and flavor profiles; they can also both make you sick to your stomach if you overindulge. Here are some of the most common types of alcohol you'll encounter in this book.

Gin
Gin is a distilled spirit flavored with botanicals, most notably juniper berries, and has a unique flavor profile. Snoop Dogg enjoys his with juice—but gin is also perfect for creating cocktails with distinctive herbal and floral notes, like a Gin and Tonic, Martini, or Negroni.

Whiskey
Most people have heard of whiskey thanks to Drag Queen Summer Glamp, the 2021 ad campaign for Jack Daniel's starring BeBe Zahara Benet, Trinity the Tuck, and Manila Luzon. But this distilled spirit, made from fermented grains like barley, corn, rye, or wheat, has actually been around for a long time—and is great for creating booze-forward cocktails like the Manhattan, Old Fashioned, and Whiskey Sour. With its strong flavor profile—which varies greatly depending on the type of grain used, the distillation method, and the aging process—whiskey (a category that includes Scotch and bourbon) can also be enjoyed neat or on the rocks.

Tequila and mezcal
Tequila and mezcal are distilled spirits made from the agave plant, with tequila specifically made from blue agave and mezcal referring to liquors made from any variety. They're commonly used in cocktails like the Margarita, Paloma, and Mezcal Negroni and can add smoky, earthy, and vegetal notes to a drink.

Rum and cachaça

Rum is distilled from molasses, a byproduct of sugar production. Commonly associated with cocktails throughout the Caribbean and Latin America, rum can add a sweet and fruity note to a drink. It's often used as a base spirit in the types of cocktails you want to be sipping poolside with a tiny umbrella garnish, like the Daiquiri, Mojito, and Mai Tai. Spiced rum has been infused with various spices, such as cinnamon, vanilla, and cloves, to give it a distinct taste. Cachaça, a close relative of rum, is made from fermented sugarcane juice and comes from Brazil, where it's famously used in Caipirinhas.

Vodka

Vodka is a clear spirit typically made from grains or potatoes and is used to create a wide diversity of cocktails, from Martinis to Bloody Marys. Its neutral flavor makes it super versatile, so it's often used for its ability to blend well with other flavors without adding much of its own character to the drink.

Brandy

Brandy (a category that includes cognac) is a spirit distilled from wine or fermented fruit, usually grapes. It's often used in classic drinks like the Sidecar and Brandy Alexander due to its rich, fruity flavor and complexity.

Liqueurs, vermouth, digestifs, and aperitifs

Liqueurs are often used in cocktails to add sweetness, flavor, and complexity, such as Baileys in a Mudslide or amaretto in an Amaretto Sour. Vermouth is commonly used as a key ingredient in classic cocktails like the Martini or Negroni, providing herbal and aromatic notes. Digestifs like Fernet-Branca and Chartreuse are enjoyed neat or used sparingly in cocktails to add a strong, distinctive flavor, while aperitifs like Campari and Aperol are often mixed with other ingredients to create refreshing pre-dinner drinks like the Aperol Spritz or the Negroni ... Sbagliato ... with prosecco in it. Oh, stunning!

Garnishes and Rims

Garnishes and rims provide concentrated flavors and visual flourishes and can transform even the most basic cocktail into drinkable art. What's not to love about a nicely done rim job?

Citrus

Citrus is the most common type of cocktail garnish and can come in all sorts of slices, wheels, wedges, and twists, adding a wallop of flavor, aroma, and visual appeal to your drink. Limes, lemons, and oranges are the most often utilized examples, but feel free to experiment the next time you have a leftover sudachi, oroblanco, or kumquat lying around. To make a wheel, cut a thin, circular slice from a citrus fruit using a sharp knife. To make a twist, cut a thin strip of the fruit's rind with a sharp knife, then bend or twist the strip over the drink to release the citrus oils before dropping it into the cocktail as a garnish.

Fruit

Use berries, cherries, melons, or any other seasonal fruit to add color, sweetness, and style to your drink. They can be used as a garnish on the rim, muddled to release their juices, or skewered on a cocktail pick. Or why not hollow out a watermelon and use it as a punch bowl? Fewer dishes to wash!

Pickled vegetables

Pickled vegetable garnishes are usually soaked in a mixture of vinegar, salt, and sugar and are used to add a welcome tangy, savory flavor and unique texture to specific cocktails. If your Bloody Mary doesn't come with something pickled, leave the brunch table immediately, Mary!

Herbs

Herbal Garnishes would make a pretty good drag name—but they also provide a range of flavors, from refreshing and herbaceous to earthy and aromatic. Common herbs used in cocktail making include mint, basil, rosemary, thyme, and cilantro (coriander), all of which can help complement or contrast with the flavors in a drink.

Edible flowers

Edible flowers can be safely consumed and add a unique visual element and subtle floral flavor. You can use them as garnishes on top of a cocktail or even crush them up and add them to your rim. Stick a whole bouquet of flowers in there! Coat your glass in moss! With foliage, you're limited only by your own creativity (and sensitivity to certain pollens).

Rims

A cocktail's rim is the outer edge of a glass that has been coated with various ingredients, such as salt, sugar, or spices, to add flavor. Rims are typically used to enhance the overall taste of a drink and can also provide a creative touch to its presentation. To rim a glass, pour a layer of your rimming mixture of choice onto a plate, wet the edge of your glass using a citrus wedge, and then dip the rim into the coating. A good rim job can involve the entire outer edge of a glass, or just a portion.

Umbrellas, straws, and other inedibles

Use tiny umbrellas, swizzle sticks, and straws to add an element of whimsy and creativity to your cocktail. They can help perfectly tailor your drink to a specific theme or occasion (see: the penis straw in Yvie Oddly's drink).

Dietary Restrictions

Some cocktails include ingredients you may want, or need, to avoid. Fortunately, there are excellent substitutes for almost any situation. Here are common swaps you can make.

Non-alcoholic spirits

With dozens of new zero-proof brands hitting the market, many of which mimic spirits like gin, whiskey, and rum, non-alcoholic beverages are having a moment in cocktail culture. They are typically made using a blend of botanicals and extracts to provide a unique and distinctive taste profile and can be used in the same way as traditional spirits. These days, even the most casual of cocktail bars has a list of delicious, complex, flavorful drinks that rival their boozy counterparts.

Vegan

Vegans should be aware that some cocktails contain animal products, such as honey or eggs. Mixers and garnishes may also include animal-derived ingredients, and some brands of alcohol might use animal products during production. Checking labels is the best way to ensure that a drink is vegan-friendly.

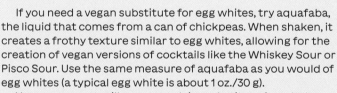

If you need a vegan substitute for egg whites, try aquafaba, the liquid that comes from a can of chickpeas. When shaken, it creates a frothy texture similar to egg whites, allowing for the creation of vegan versions of cocktails like the Whiskey Sour or Pisco Sour. Use the same measure of aquafaba as you would of egg whites (a typical egg white is about 1 oz./30 g).

You can use oat milk as a non-dairy substitute for whole milk in cocktails; it provides a similarly creamy texture along with a slightly sweeter flavor. Bartenders often shake or froth oat milk to create a smooth consistency similar to dairy milk.

Gluten-free alcohol and mixers

For someone who has a gluten allergy, you'll need to make sure your ingredients are gluten-free. Most beers aren't, but fortunately most hard liquors made from wheat and barley are considered gluten-free as long as they have been distilled. Still, check your labels and make sure nothing has been added to the booze that might be gluten-based.

Nut allergies

Cinnamon or allspice can be used as a substitute for nutmeg, adjusting the quantity to taste. Orgeat syrup is usually made from almonds, but if you need to, you can use a commercial version that is specifically labeled as nut-free, or substitute maple syrup, honey, or simple syrup.

Kim Chi

Donut Come for Me

For the strawberry-and-kimchi purée (makes 4 shots)
- ⅓ cup (50 g) strawberries
- ¼ cup (40 g) mild kimchi

Add ingredients to a blender and purée until smooth.

For the cocktail
- 2 shots gin
- 1 shot Aperol
- 1 shot strawberry-and-kimchi purée
- 1 shot fresh lemon juice
Garnish: sliced kimchi on a cocktail skewer

Add all ingredients to a shaker filled with ice. Shake, strain into the tallest chilled coupe glass you can find, and garnish. Pair with a sprinkle donut.

The next time you're in a CVS Pharmacy picking up deodorant (or doxycycline), keep your eyes peeled for hydrating mint lip gloss from KimChi Chic Beauty. The brand's founder, drag-queen-cum-businesswoman Kim Chi, has spun her star performance on season eight of *RuPaul's Drag Race* into several successful entrepreneurial endeavors. In addition to her beauty line—which includes essentials like a vegan fake-freckle appliqué—Kim Chi also launched her own package of emojis, called Kimchiji. They help fill some glaring omissions in the traditional emoji keyboard, like a spanked butt cheek, a bottle of sriracha, and (of course) a heaping pile of kimchi.

Raised in both the United States and South Korea, Kim Chi is among the most popular performers to have burst out of the *Drag Race* multiverse, boasting millions of Instagram followers. A self-described "live-action anime character," "high-fashion model," and "bionic doily," Kim Chi is best known for her high-concept drag. Previous looks have taken inspiration from silent film-era clowns, and from imagining what the late magazine editor Isabella Blow might have worn to a funeral (think *Beetlejuice* meets *Æon Flux*).

Kim Chi also celebrates her Korean roots in much of her drag. One of her most iconic outfits, worn during her *Drag Race* finale performance in 2016, was a take on a traditional Korean *hanbok*. This gin-based cocktail with strawberry-and-kimchi purée pays homage to her heritage as well, and is named for her fondness for pastry-based puns. "Do-nut come for me!" she deadpanned to the camera during a season eight confessional while holding, yes, a donut, "or I will destroy you!" Make sure to serve the Donut Come for Me in the tallest coupe you can find: this queen stands *seven feet tall* in heels.

Monét X Change

This is one queen whose stock has *soared* since her initial public offering on season ten of *Drag Race* in 2018. "I'm Monét X Change," she proclaimed to the world, before issuing an astute—if unsolicited—piece of financial advice: "You better get your currency in check, bitch."

Monét has been busy counting plenty of her own coin since winning *Drag Race All Stars* season four in 2019 alongside her "twinner" Trinity the Tuck—the first double win in the show's history. She went on to host her own online talk show, *The X Change Rate*, produced by Yahoo! Each episode starts with Monét offering really bad financial advice ("the best way to save money is to forget who you borrowed it from") and ends with interviews with the likes of Iggy Azalea, Cecily Strong, and Ts Madison. She also hosts two podcasts: *Sibling Rivalry*, alongside Bob the Drag Queen, and *Ebony and Irony* with Lady Bunny, which covers "all the news unfit to print."

Monét is a classically trained opera singer, but she largely hid the skill from her adoring public until a talent contest segment of *All Stars* in 2022. Her rendition of "Vi ravviso, luoghi ameni" from the opera *La Sonnambula*, sung in her baritone-bass vibrato, dropped the jaws of the judges and her fellow queens. She "has had a lot of things inside of her," quipped fellow contestant Jaida Essence Hall during a testimonial after the performance, "but we didn't know this was one of them." After displaying her talents on the show, Monét went on to make her operatic debut proper—in drag!—with the Minnesota Opera. She is also a member of the LA Opera Legacy Ambassador Program, which works to introduce the art form to communities of color.

Shockingly, despite single-handedly resuscitating the cultural significance of the Scotch-Brite brand thanks to the iconically tragic "sponge dress" she made during a *Drag Race* design challenge, Monét has yet to sign an endorsement deal with the cleaning company. Hopefully, this take on the melon-flavored Midori Sour, created to toast this queen—complete with a lemon-lime sponge garnish—will do in the meantime.

Sponge Tart

- 1 shot Midori
- 1 shot vodka
- 2 shots club soda (soda water)
- ½ shot fresh lemon juice
- ½ shot fresh lime juice
Garnish: lemon and lime half-wheels

Add all ingredients to a rocks glass with one large ice cube, stir, and garnish with lemon and lime half-wheels (a citrus sponge!) on a cocktail pick.

Annie Hindle

On a summer day in June 1886, a Baptist minister stood before two women in Grand Rapids, Michigan, and performed one of the USA's first known same-sex wedding ceremonies. The minister was not, however, some shockingly woke early advocate for marriage equality—they had simply been duped by the convincing drag of the one and only Annie Hindle, widely considered the first major male impersonator in the United States.

Annie's drag career started in music halls in London, where she performed as both male and female characters. But after moving stateside, her act consisted entirely of male drag. She quickly became the best-known male impersonator of the era to perform on the American variety stage. Gender-bending was new at the time for US audiences, but Annie managed to win over her mostly working-class crowd with her quick wit, songs about courting women, and impersonations of pretentious upper-class men. At the peak of her fame, she was one of the highest-paid vaudeville performers in the country.

Annie was also the subject of public intrigue due to her many marriages. She wed four separate times throughout her life, twice to men and twice to women. A reporter once marveled, toward the end of her career, that she was the only person alive to have been "a wife, a widow, a husband, a widower, and again a husband." Though her marriages to women were scandalous for the time (and led some to suspect she was, in fact, a cisgender man), she still managed to work consistently throughout four decades.

A reviewer once described Annie's low alto singing voice as having a "vim and dash that was really refreshing." The same could be said about this drink, concocted in celebration of Annie. A take on the Moscow Mule, this cocktail trades out vodka for absinthe, a type of anise-flavored booze with supposed hallucinogenic effects that was all the rage in her day. After a couple of these bad boys, gender might not be the only thing you'll see bending.

Wife, Widow, Husband, Widower

- 1 shot absinthe
- ½ shot fresh lime juice
- 2 shots champagne
- 2 shots ginger beer
Garnish: mint sprigs

Add absinthe and lime juice to a shaker filled with ice. Shake, then strain into an old-fashioned coupe glass filled with crushed ice. Top with champagne and ginger beer, and stir. Garnish with 4 sprigs of mint (one for each marriage!) and serve with a straw.

Dina Martina

Just like her favorite catchphrase, this queen is "off the charts!" and completely off the rails. If you gave a sedated clown a microphone after she'd undergone major dental surgery, you'd have something similar—but still inferior—to the Dina Martina experience. As one audience member put it in an online review, "I thought there was something seriously wrong with her face." It can be difficult to understand what Dina says sometimes due to her refusal to pronounce her hard G's, but thankfully she hasn't let this random speech flourish stop her from "jifting" audiences with her best approximation of a singing voice since the late 1980s. Every now and then, she even hits the right note!

Dina isn't like the other girls (or humans, really)—which is exactly what's kept fans flocking to her residency in Provincetown, Massachusetts, every summer since 2004. Crowning herself the Second Lady of Entertainment, Dina is the rare queen who manages to turn drag into high art (meaning she may well be high while performing). Equal parts cabaret act and freak show, a Dina Martina performance is packed with, as her website says, "ludicrous song, horrifying stories, and overburdened costumes." Apart from her permanent camel toe, she's perhaps best known for her Christmas shows, her vibrato warbling like a walrus in heat through renditions of "Away in a Manger" and "Angels We Have Heard on High."

A true triple threat, Dina doesn't just sing and dance badly—she acts poorly, too. Her shows often include short, wackadoodle films featuring her gruff-voiced best friend Doreen, or her own head superimposed on top of *Jeopardy!* contestants or presidential candidates. Should you go see her live? "If you have all the time in the world!" Dina would say. The same goes for whether you should make the cocktail inspired by this beloved trainwreck of a queen, which features one of her favorite foods as a garnish: the cocktail weenie.

Priyanka

When this queen introduces herself, be sure to listen up, because there *will* be a pop quiz afterwards. "My name is Priyanka," she'll say to anyone who'll listen, immediately followed by, "*What's* my name?" It's a gimmick, she admits, but one with a purpose: Priyanka chose her moniker so that, whenever she performs, audiences know there's "an Indo-queer West Indian queen coming onstage," as she once told *Elle* Canada.

Born Mark Suknanan, the man behind Priyanka got his start as a performer in the same way as most drag queens: as the presenter of a children's television show. Over the course of eight years, he hosted programs (out of drag) on Canada's YTV network, like *The Zone* and *The Next Star*. After hiring a drag queen to perform at his twenty-sixth birthday, however, Mark was inspired to shed his family-friendly television persona and succumbed to the Drag Dark Arts. And thus, Priyanka was born.

Drag is typically known as an art form requiring many years of blood, sweat, tucking, and tears before performers reach anything close to mainstream success—but not so for Priyanka. Within two years of hitting Toronto's scene, she went from an unknown little drag baby to Toronto's top queen, at least according to *Now*, an alternative online mag based in the city. Soon after, Mama Ru came calling, casting Priyanka in the first season of *Canada's Drag Race* in 2020. Despite having the least amount of experience compared to her fellow racers, Priyanka won the crown.

Her success has garnered her a global touring career, legions of fans, and even more opportunities to return to the small screen. In 2022, Netflix cast Priyanka as a guest star on *Glamorous*, a comedy about a New York-based cosmetics company, alongside Kim Cattrall and fellow *Drag Race* alum Monét X Change. That same year, she filmed an episode of *Ezra*, a show on OUTtv about queer vampires.

Priyanka is clearly just getting started. But, quick: *what's* her name? Lest you forget, shake up a batch of this tasty apple-based cocktail—it's packed with so much vitamin C it'll be sure to jog your memory.

What's Her Name?

- 2 shots spiced rum
- ½ shot amaretto
- 2 tsp maple syrup
- 2 dashes Angostura bitters
- 2 shots hard cider
Garnish: sliced apple

Add rum, amaretto, maple syrup, and bitters to a shaker filled with ice. Shake, strain into a highball glass filled with crushed ice, and top with hard cider. Stir and garnish with 2 apple slices. Serve with a straw. Raise your glass to toast ... whatever her name is.

Christeene

Blue-Eyed Gutter Slut

For the lychee eyeball garnish
- 1 lychee, pit removed
- ¼ tsp cherry preserves (jam)
- 1 blueberry

Fill the lychee with cherry preserves, then place a blueberry in the cavity.

For the cocktail
- 1 shot Goldschläger
- ½ shot blue curaçao
- ½ shot Jägermeister
- Garnish: lychee eyeball

Add Goldschläger to a double shot glass, then slowly pour in blue curaçao and watch it sink to the bottom. For the final layer, add Jägermeister on top by carefully pouring it over the back of a spoon. Garnish by violently skewering the lychee eyeball with a cocktail pick and laying it across the rim of the glass, then enjoy—if you dare.

This spooky queen, birthed from the twisted brains of Paul Soileau, has been variously described as a "drag terrorist," "Beyoncé on bath salts," and a "gutter slut" since first emerging from her cocoon back in 2010. The individual pieces of Christeene's trademark look—tattered clothes, smeared makeup, and alien-blue contact lenses—culminate in the type of creature children fear might be living under their beds at night, like a slightly more glam version of the girl from *The Ring*.

During a Christeene performance, you may find yourself dodging dildos affixed to balloons ("a gift" to her audiences, she explains) or being directed to "love one another's buttholes." She is unabashedly hypersexual, queer, and feral—and doesn't give a fuck if you get what she's trying to do or not. It's an attitude that has made her the perfect collaborator for fellow potty-mouthed raconteur, the musician Peaches. (Do yourself a favor—break out your best pearl necklace to clutch and then google some of their duets.)

Christeene has gifted the world several recorded albums. Her 2012 debut, *Waste Up, Kneez Down*, includes toe-tappers like "Fix My Dick" and "Tears from My Pussy." She released her sophomore album, *Basura*, in 2018, followed by *Midnite Fukk Train* in 2022. She also frequently collaborates with queer filmmaker PJ Raval to create music videos. The video for her song "Butt Muscle" features Christeene urinating into Rick Owens's open mouth. It was the famed fashion designer's idea, apparently—he's just one of the many fans who claim Christeene as their muse.

For all her shock value, Christeene is not really out to make you blush. Rather, she's asking you to join her in giving the middle finger to all things conformist, heteronormative, and boring. She's providing you a safe space in which you, too, can let loose the little demon living inside you. Because no matter how freaky-deaky your inner child may be, it will never be weirder than hers.

The beverage created in Christeene's honor, the Blue-Eyed Gutter Slut—named after her stunning blue irises and the fact that she's a slut—may not look safe to drink. But not to worry, this cocktail is one-hundo-percent potable … probably.

Manila Luzon

Fruit Queen Supreme

- 1½ shots light rum
- ¾ shot triple sec (Cointreau)
- ½ shot dark rum
- 1 shot orgeat syrup
- 1 shot pineapple juice
- ¾ shot fresh lime juice
Garnish: pineapple leaves and maraschino cherries

Add all ingredients to a shaker filled with ice. Shake, then strain into a hollowed-out pineapple filled with ice. (Or just a pineapple-etched Hurricane glass if you're feeling lazy.) Garnish and serve with a straw.

Karl Philip Michael and Clark Joseph Kent have a suspicious number of things in common. Both are known by three of the most basic boy names in the English language, but when the tights come on, these queens undergo *quite* the transformation (and no one has ever seen Manila Luzon and Superman in the same room at the same time—just saying). Truthfully, Ms. Kent could never reach the soaring heights of this stunning queen, who can turn a look inspired by a pineapple, a box of popcorn, or Big Bird into glamorous, campy perfection.

Manila competed on the third season of *Drag Race* in 2011 as well as the first and fourth seasons of *All Stars*, in 2012 and 2018. Though she has never earned the crown, to her adoring audiences across the globe, who call themselves "Fanilas," she's true royalty. Since her time on the show, Manila has become something of a drag darling for brands like Maybelline, Jack Daniel's, and Bubly Sparkling Water. Disney even hired her to transform herself into *Cruella*'s eponymous villainess to help promote the release of the movie in 2021.

In 2023, Manila—whose name is taken from the Philippines' capital city, where her mother was born—began hosting her own competition show, *Drag Den*, on Amazon Prime Video. The series, the first of its kind in the Philippines, showcases the talents of eight performers, all vying for the extremely coveted title of Filipino Drag Supreme. "Drag in the Philippines is the best in the world," said Manila in an interview, continuing, "I'm so proud to showcase them."

There is *no* queen fruitier than the one and only Manila Luzon. Thanks to her trademark pineapple dress, she has become synonymous with the tropical fruit. Her look—which has already inspired a collection of dolls, a "Fineapple Couture" clothing line, and Halloween costumes—has now resulted in the ultimate accolade: this sweet pineapple drink designed in her image.

Murray Hill

Murray Hill is the "hardest working middle-aged man in show business," according to his website; he has been delighting audiences since "before Zendaya was alive."

Murray got his start in the 1990s impersonating a "fat, sweaty Elvis" at a drag king party called Club Casanova in Manhattan's East Village. He developed his persona by mixing together aspects of comedian Benny Hill, the character Jack from the TV show *Three's Company*, and his own "chubby, cute, short" Italian grandfather. An old-school performer fond of proclaiming "Showbiz!" at random moments during his act, Murray's self-deprecating humor and cheesy schtick have earned him a dedicated following—so much so that, in 2022, when his Brooklyn home burned to the ground (on his fiftieth birthday, no less), a GoFundMe set up to help him and his neighbors quickly raised more than $100,000.

Before his glitzy showbiz days, Murray actually made a go at a political career. In 1996, he waged a spirited but ultimately unsuccessful campaign against former mayor (and current sock puppet) Rudy Giuliani, running a campaign on the "drag king ticket" that was equal parts performance art and protest. "My platform was 'Let the Kids Dance,'" he said in an interview—a not-so-subtle rebuke to Giuliani's *Footloose*-esque crusade against (most often queer) nightlife.

These days, Murray continues to stay true to his East Village roots, regularly selling out crowds at storied venue Joe's Pub. But he's also vastly expanded the reach of his monarchy: on the small screen, you can find him starring alongside the likes of Bridget Everett in HBO's *Somebody, Somewhere* and Amy Schumer in Hulu's *Life & Beth*. Murray continues to be a much-sought-after emcee for concerts and cameos—this icon pops up in the videos and projects of everyone from Le Tigre to the Beastie Boys.

Just like Murray Hill, this refreshing beverage tips its hat toward tradition, with some modern *pizzazz*, baby! The Mister Showbiz is a take on a Rusty Nail, the drink of choice for the Rat Pack boys, but swaps out Scotch for mezcal.

Mister Showbiz

- 1½ shots mezcal
- ¾ shot Drambuie
- ¼ shot (1½ tsp) fresh lemon juice
- Splash of ginger beer
Garnish: lemon twist

Add all ingredients to a rocks glass with one large ice cube, stir, and garnish. Enjoy with a cigar—and that's *showbiz*, mister!

Bianca Del Rio

Louisiana-born Bianca Del Rio was already a well-known quantity in clubs from New York to New Orleans before she won the sixth season of *RuPaul's Drag Race* in 2014. Today, with multiple world tours under her belt, a *Hurricane Bianca* movie franchise, and a successful run in a West End musical, she's among the best-known queens in the world, selling out shows from Carnegie Hall to Wembley Arena.

In 2021, *New York* magazine dubbed Bianca the "most powerful queen" out of one hundred former *Drag Race* contestants—and her strength stems directly from her filthy little mouth. Though she describes herself as an "erotic clown," she's an insult comic at heart, as sharp-tongued as Lily Savage and as bitchy as Triumph the Insult Comic Dog. "She's kind of grown on me," Bianca once said of fellow season six contestant Gia Gunn, adding, "like a rash."

Despite the jabs that other queens and audience members have come to expect from Bianca, she's just as quick to train her wit on herself. "I'm the biggest joke there is," she said during an interview. "If you can't laugh at yourself, how the hell are you going to laugh at anybody else?"

The *New York Times* once deemed Bianca "the Joan Rivers of the drag world"—a fitting comparison, since Bianca cites Ms. Rivers as one of her inspirations. Before the reigning "queen of mean" died in 2014, the two even became friends in real life. "Is this the first time Joan has fucked a clown?" Bianca asked as a guest on the YouTube series *In Bed with Joan* (literally filmed in Joan's bed), "We'll find out!"

Bianca is fond of banishing demons with her catchphrase "Not today, Satan!" But after a couple of these cocktails, it may finally be the devil's day. This wicked, blended take on the classic Hurricane pays homage to the favorite rum-soaked drink of Bianca's hometown, as well as her movies. Don't forget to add an umbrella—this is one queen who prefers the shade.

Bob the Drag Queen

Tea Bag First*

For the apple purse garnish
• 1 green apple

Cut two quarter-inch (6 mm) slices from the apple. Shape one into a rectangle and the other into a half-moon. Fasten the pieces together with a toothpick.

For the drink
• 1 Earl Grey tea bag
• 1 white tea bag
• 1–2 tbsp honey (to taste)
• 1 peach, pitted and sliced
• 8 sprigs thyme
Garnish: green apple purse and a sprig of thyme

Bring 2 cups (480 ml) water to a boil. Turn off heat, add tea bags, and steep for 3 to 5 minutes. Stir in honey. Transfer to a pitcher and chill. In a bowl, muddle the sliced peach and thyme (stems removed) until smooth. Add to the chilled tea, stir, pour into a Collins glass filled with ice, and garnish.

* This is a zero-proof cocktail.

Drag legends, like superheroes and fast-food mascots, are nothing without their catchphrases, and Bob the Drag Queen has among the most memorable. With all the clubs this queen has sashayed into "purse first" since winning season eight of *Drag Race* in 2016, her arm must be getting tired.

Drag has been a part of Bob's life since long before she donned her first pair of heels. When she was a child, her mother, Martha, owned a drag bar called Sensations in Columbus, Georgia. On nights when Martha couldn't afford a babysitter, a young Bob—nary a purse to his name—worked the door.

Bob is, in her own words, "hilarious, beautiful, talented, and humble"—and a standout comedy queen. "It's my dad's name," she'll say, when asked about her alias, following with, "My dad's name is 'The Drag Queen.'" Her quick wit has earned her spots on TV shows like *High Maintenance* and *A Black Lady Sketch Show*, and her own Netflix special, *Suspiciously Large Woman*. Still, she gets serious when the occasion calls for it. In 2011, the NYPD arrested Bob for blocking a road while protesting in favor of marriage equality, throwing her in jail in full drag. According to Bob, it makes sense that drag artists are at the forefront of campaigns for justice. Drag is like "armor," she said, allowing queens to "get out in front."

Alongside fellow *Drag Race* alums Shangela and Eureka O'Hara, Bob stars in the Emmy-nominated HBO show *We're Here*, which follows the trio as they stage drag shows in small-town USA. In an episode filmed in Selma, Alabama, the queens met with a group of Black women and civil rights leaders who faced brutal attacks while peacefully walking across the Edmund Pettus Bridge in 1965. Bob dedicated her performance during this episode—which involved hiding her entire eleven-year-old niece *inside her afro*—to her ability to even perform today as a queer, nonbinary, Black drag queen.

This sweet, peachy concoction pays homage to Bob's Southern roots, while using the cocktail version of a purse —a tea bag, duh.

Divine

During the 1970s, when drag was more about "passing" and pageantry, Divine struck a decidedly unladylike figure. In the words of John Waters, the queer film director and her creative partner, she was the "Godzilla of drag queens."

The most notorious example of Divine's inelegance, of course, comes from Waters's film *Pink Flamingos* (1972), in which she eats literal dog poop. The movie caused such a shit storm that it was banned in several countries. So, why did Divine eat actual dog excrement instead of fake poop? "It was in the script," the consummate professional explained. She was so committed to her performance, in fact, that she followed a dog around for three hours, "zooming in on its asshole," until it relieved itself.

We'd be shitting all over this queen's legacy were we to end the discussion here. The collaboration between Divine and Waters led to too many beautifully chaotic cinematic moments to mention. In *Hairspray* (1988), we get Divine's version of a shut-in housewife: "I've got nothin' but hampers of ironing to do," Edna Turnblad moans, "and my diet pill is wearing off." In *Female Trouble* (1974), we're gifted her take on a bratty teenager, Dawn, who topples a Christmas tree in a blind rage over cha-cha heels.

Ultimately, Divine's legacy is the space she created for an entirely new generation of oddballs—once you quite literally eat shit, you can't possibly get any weirder. Everyone from Beth Ditto to RuPaul has cited her as a muse. Still, Divine's best-known drag daughter is none other than Ursula, the voluptuous octo-witch from *The Little Mermaid* (1989)—illustrator Rob Minkoff has cited this queen as a major source of inspiration for Disney's most campy villainess.

The cocktail created to honor this unrivaled legend is a fresh take on the Pink Squirrel, a popular drink from Divine's day. The beverage also has a rosy hue, a nod to the pink of her most iconic film. Don't worry, though, that brown stuff floating on top is just nutmeg. (Or is it?)

Pink Puppy

- ¾ shot crème de noyaux
- ¾ shot white crème de cacao
- 1½ shots heavy (double or whipping) cream
Garnish: fresh nutmeg

Add all ingredients to a shaker filled with ice. Shake, then strain into a chilled coupe glass. Garnish with freshly grated nutmeg—unless you *really* want to show your devotion and have three hours to spare.

Jinkx Monsoon

This queen, a self-described "internationally tolerated" cabaret icon, is an amalgamation of various divas from the small and silver screens. Take the vanity of Meryl Streep and Goldie Hawn in *Death Becomes Her*, mix in a dollop of clueless Edina from *Absolutely Fabulous*, and top it off with the wacky humor of Lucille Ball—and you have yourself the one and only mother-tucking Jinkx Monsoon.

Jinkx is, without question, among the most legendary queens birthed from the fertile loins of *Drag Race*. She holds the distinction of being the only contestant to win the competition not once but *twice*: triumphing in seasons five and seven of *Drag Race* and *All Stars*, respectively. Like many queens before her, Jinkx released music following her stint on the show (her first record, 2014's *The Inevitable Album*, pokes fun at this well-trodden tradition). Unlike many of her sisters, however, Jinkx is a trained singer: no Auto-Tune for this diva! She's one half of the cabaret duo The Vaudevillians, a 1920s-inspired revival act that she performs alongside pianist Major Scales. In 2023 she landed a role on Broadway, making her the first drag queen to take on the part of Matron "Mama" Morton in *Chicago*.

Much like her idol Lucille Ball, Jinkx is also a comedienne, with several of the most hilarious Snatch Game celebrity impersonation performances in *Drag Race* herstory under her belt. During her first season, she schooled a new generation of gaybies on the camp sensibilities of Edith Bouvier Beale, or "Little Edie" from *Grey Gardens* (1975). During *All Stars* in 2022, she flawlessly mimicked the husky-voiced Natasha Lyonne before transforming herself into a bewildered Judy Garland; a clip of her singing RuPaul's song "Jealous of My Boogie"—in character—went viral after the show.

Jinkx no longer drinks, a decision she says—combined with therapy, witchcraft, and her mantra, "water off a duck's back"—has gotten her to a "pretty solid place." Still, she's "California sober," so this refreshing beverage—a dry version of a Moscow Mule—sprinkles in a couple drops of THC or CBD. Best enjoyed while plunging deep into a Jinkx Monsoon YouTube rabbit hole.

Water Off a Mule's Back*

- 1½ shots fresh orange juice
- 1½ shots fresh lime juice
- 1 shot honey syrup (p. 15)
- THC or CBD drops, to taste
- 1 pinch cayenne pepper
- 1½ shots ginger beer

Garnish: sprig of mint and a lime wheel

Add orange juice, lime juice, honey syrup, THC or CBD drops, and cayenne pepper to a shaker filled with ice. Shake, then strain into an ice-filled Mule glass. Top with ginger beer, stir, and garnish.

* This is a zero-proof cocktail (but contains THC or CBD).

Stormé DeLarverie

Dark 'n' Stormé

For the rhubarb syrup
• 2 cups (200 g) chopped rhubarb
• 2 tbsp sugar

Place ingredients in a saucepan with 1 cup (240 ml) water. Stir over low heat until rhubarb begins to fall apart (6 to 8 minutes). Strain and let cool.

For the cocktail
• 1 lime wedge
• 1½ shots spiced rum
• 2 shots ginger beer
• 1½ shots rhubarb syrup

Squeeze lime wedge into a highball glass and add to the glass. Fill with ice and add rum, ginger beer, and rhubarb syrup. Stir and serve with a straw. Enjoy while patrolling the neighborhood, looking for trouble.

Many believe this drag king was the first person to throw a punch at the Stonewall Inn during the 1969 uprising. True or not, the LGBTQ activism bona fides of Stormé DeLarverie (which she said should be pronounced "Stormy De-Lah-vee-ay") have never been in question. Known as the "guardian of the lesbians" in Greenwich Village, Stormé patrolled the area's queer bars from the 1980s to the 2000s (when she was well into her eighties!), armed with a permitted gun, looking for signs of trouble. "I can spot ugly in a minute," she said in a 2009 interview. "They'll just walk away, and that's a good thing to do because I'll either pick up the phone or I'll nail you."

Born in 1920 to a wealthy white man and a Black woman who worked as his servant, the androgynous Stormé could pass for Black or white, male or female. She started singing in her teens, booking gigs first presenting as a woman and later as a man. In the 1950s, she began working with the famed drag troupe the Jewel Box Revue as its only male impersonator; the cabaret's tagline was "25 men and one girl." Thanks to her "deep baritone voice," audiences never suspected she was the "one girl" in the show, according to reviews of the time. Stormé performed with the group for fourteen years, appearing onstage at some of New York's most famous venues, like the Apollo Theater and Radio City Music Hall, among many others around the country.

Later in life, Stormé took up residence at New York's famed Chelsea Hotel and worked security for two of the city's legendary (and still standing) lesbian bars, Cubbyhole and Henrietta Hudson. She thought of herself less as a "bouncer," she said, than as a "babysitter of my people, all the boys and girls." Lisa Cannistraci, the longtime owner of Henrietta Hudson, said Stormé would walk the streets of downtown Manhattan like a "gay superhero—she was not to be messed with by any stretch of the imagination."

Stormé puckered a lip or two in her day, and so will this sour cocktail: a take on the Dark 'n' Stormy created in her honor.

Katya Zamolodchikova

Russian Ding-Dong*

- 2 tbsp instant coffee granules
- 2 tbsp granulated sugar
- 1 shot coffee syrup
- 1 splash vanilla extract
- 1 shot heavy (double or whipping) cream

Using an electric mixer, whip together 1 shot of hot water, instant coffee granules, and sugar in a bowl until fluffy (2 to 3 minutes). Add coffee syrup and vanilla extract to a rocks glass filled with ice and stir. Slowly pour in cream to create a second layer. Add whipped coffee mixture on top. Serve with a spoon and a pair of stainless steel slip-joint pliers.

* This is a zero-proof cocktail.

Lest you be bamboozled by this queen's convincing accent, the performer behind Katya Zamolodchikova, Brian McCook, is decidedly not Russian—he's from Marlborough, Massachusetts. He is, however, a huge fan of languages and used a cassette tape called *Pronounce It Perfectly* to help master the accent. The idea for the character came from one of Brian's professors, who "never left the house without a full face of makeup" and wore "six-inch stilettos in the snow." It's a fitting inspiration for the self-proclaimed "sweatiest woman in show business," who shot to fame on the seventh and second seasons of *Drag Race* and *All Stars*, respectively.

Together with Trixie Mattel, Katya has produced a treasure trove of unhinged projects, including global tours, multiple web and television series, and a *New York Times* bestselling book, *Trixie and Katya's Guide to Modern Womanhood*. The pair are best known, however, for their chaotically endearing web series *UNHhhh* (which must be pronounced while caressing fake boobs). Armed with a green screen and the power of their own delusions, the queens are barely coherent—and deeply entertaining. The show is worth it for their nonsensical introductions alone ("I'm life-sized human person, Katya," or "I'm the subprime auto loan of drag, Katya").

Among the many music videos created by *Drag Race* alumni, Kayta's are standouts for their artistry and tomfoolery. She contains multitudes, and displays each of them simultaneously in the video for "Ding Dong!," which she describes as a "Eurovision nightmare dance party in Hell." In a guided meditation video titled "Be Your Own Dentist," meanwhile, Katya softly purrs: "You won't need anything special for this exercise, other than your body, your breath, and a pair of stainless steel slip-joint pliers."

Just like Katya, this caffeinated drink—a take on the dalgona whipped coffee trend—is made from cheap ingredients you likely already have in your pantry. So dust off that canister of instant coffee you haven't touched since the pandemic and toast this true artist and inspiration!

Lady Bunny

Wig and Tonic*

- ½ shot fresh grapefruit juice
- ½ shot white cranberry peach juice (substitute: peach juice)
- ½ shot fresh lime juice
- 2 shots club soda (soda water)
- 1 shot tonic water
Garnish: cotton candy (candy floss), to taste

Add grapefruit juice, cranberry peach juice, and lime juice to a shaker filled with ice. Shake, then strain into a wide coupe glass. Top with club soda and tonic, and stir. Garnish with an artfully placed "puff" of cotton candy.

* This is a zero-proof cocktail.

Lady Bunny is instantly recognizable thanks to her trademark blond bouffant, which has gotten slightly bigger each year since she donned her first wig in Atlanta, Georgia, in the early 1980s. That's also where she first met a fellow queen by the name of RuPaul. The two briefly worked together as go-go dancers for a band called Now Explosion before moving to New York City in 1983. They honed their drag personas as roommates, while simultaneously laying the groundwork for global domination.

RuPaul, of course, emerged decades later as a household name and the One True Overlady of the Drag Dark Arts. But Lady Bunny also elevated the art form's place in the zeitgeist thanks to Wigstock, a yearly drag festival she co-founded and emceed. She first conceived the idea in 1985 after she and some fellow queens drunkenly stumbled out of the Pyramid Club on Avenue A and into neighboring Tompkins Square Park, where they put on a show for whatever weirdos happened to be gathered that night. In the years that followed, legends like Amanda Lepore, Crystal Waters, Deee-Lite, Debbie Harry, Leigh Bowery, and RuPaul all graced Wigstock's stage.

While her famous former roommate has spun herself into a drag oracle, Lady Bunny has stayed remarkably consistent to her insult-laden, East Village roots. Her shows have always been—and always will be—packed with more political incorrectness than an early 2000s Judd Apatow movie. "It's hotter than a spoon in Demi Lovato's house!" she might quip. And when the inevitable backlash comes, she'll counter, "Why have we become so politically correct? Are we going to make Dick Van Dyke change his name to Penis Van Lesbian?"

A proper toast to Lady Bunny would involve several shots of bottom-shelf liquor followed by a spontaneous performance in the nearest park with your friends. But this queen doesn't drink much these days. So instead, enjoy this fruity zero-proof cocktail topped with a giant dollop of cotton candy. Remember: the higher the candied bouffant, the closer to heaven—which is the nearest this shady queen will ever get!

Latrice Royale

Chunky-Yet-Funky Bowl

Makes 6 to 8 drinks
- 8 shots rum
- 2 shots gin
- 2 shots cognac
- 3-4 shots fresh lemon juice (to taste)
- 3 shots fresh orange juice
- 3 shots orgeat syrup
- 2 cups (400 g) crushed ice

Garnish: edible flowers, mint sprigs, maraschino cherries, cinnamon sticks, citrus peel, citrus wheels, pineapple wedges, and paper umbrellas

Add all ingredients to a blender and blend until smooth. Pour into a punch bowl filled with several large ice cubes, and garnish. Add multiple straws. Best enjoyed with Latrice's nuts.

This three-time *Drag Race* competitor, who appeared on the fourth season of *RuPaul's Drag Race* and the first and fourth seasons of *All Stars*, may never have snatched the show's crown. But Latrice Royale has nevertheless wedged herself deep in the annals of drag history.

She has released music, toured the world with her stage shows, and appeared in numerous TV shows and movies. Yet, despite her impressive résumé, Latrice's most important cultural contribution will forever be the treasure trove of one-liners she has gifted the world. At this point, entire queer friend groups communicate exclusively through Latrice memes. Is someone doing the absolute most? Chastise them with her five G's: "Good God Girl Get a Grip!" Did your best Judy land a good read in the group text? Reward them handsomely with Latrice's, "The shade, the *shade* of it all."

This entrepreneurial queen even parlayed one of her most iconic quips ("Get those nuts away from *my* face!") into a partnership with Squirrel Brand. In 2021, Latrice teamed up with the company to promote a trail mix called Ruby Royale, which was sold in bright pink packaging. She even appeared on QVC to hawk the nuts, becoming the only queen in history—besides Joan Rivers—to grace the home shopping channel in full drag regalia.

Latrice has also been among the most prominent spokespeople for body positivity to emerge from the *Drag Race* omniverse. "When you stand your ground and have integrity, it's magnetic, it's attractive," she said in an interview. "People see that I can hold myself and be proud of my size and stature, regardless of what other people think." For a 2022 social media post to promote self-acceptance as part of the online video project StyleLikeU, Latrice and her husband discussed the misconceptions they face as a mixed-race couple of different sizes, all the while stripping down to their unmentionables.

As Latrice once said, "Jesus is a biscuit! Let him sop you up!" Then wash it all down with this rum punch created to celebrate everyone's favorite "chunky yet funky" queen.

Miss Coco Peru

It Burnssssss!

- 1½ shots gin
- ¾ shot elderflower liqueur
- ¾ shot fresh lemon juice
- ½ shot egg white
  (or aquafaba)
- ½ shot green Chartreuse
Garnish: leftover egg white

Add gin, elderflower liqueur, lemon juice, and egg white into a shaker without ice and shake. Add ice, shake again, and strain into a chilled Nick and Nora glass. Pour the green Chartreuse into a handled metal measuring cup, ignite, and carefully pour the flaming Chartreuse over the top of the drink. Tastefully drip leftover egg white down the side of the glass.

This hardworking queen, instantly recognizable thanks to her flipped-out ginger wig, has written and starred in over ten one-woman shows since the early 1990s, including *Miss Coco Peru: A Legend in Progress* and *Miss Coco Peru in My Goddamn Cabaret*. During a Coco performance, audiences can expect comedy ("I'm a free prostitute on the streets of Manhattan"), belted-out Broadway numbers (swapping "Roxie Hart" for "Coco Peru," of course), and poignant anecdotes from her Bronx upbringing and career. She balances these multiple talents so seamlessly, Lily Tomlin once called her "one of the last great storytellers."

In more recent years, Coco has taken her act online. One YouTube video features her frantic search for Celestial Seasonings Tension Tamer tea, her favorite relaxing beverage. Along the way, viewers are treated to her trademark musings about the state of the world (and big-box stores). "There's too many people on the planet, why are they locking up the condoms?" she asks in a Big Lots. "Let them steal it!" Though she is ultimately unsuccessful in her quest, the video went viral, and Coco had to ask fans to stop sending her tea—she has enough now, thank you!

From 2005 to 2016 she hosted *Conversations with Coco*, a live stage show that doubled as a fundraiser for homeless LGBTQ youth. Over the years she interviewed countless seminal performers, like Bea Arthur, Liza Minnelli, and Jane Fonda—the last of whom delighted the assembled queers in the audience by saying "cock ring" onstage. But Coco's most personal guest was Charles Busch, the 1970s drag queen and playwright who inspired her own career.

Her many accolades aside, Coco's best-known performance is in the 1999 gay romcom *Trick*. Her nearly five-minute monologue stole the entire movie—and traumatized an entire generation of queer people, who will forever avoid her at all costs in bathrooms. "You ever get cum in your eye?" Coco asks the terrified lead twink as he's trying to pee, continuing, "It *burnsssss*!" It's a performance that also inspired this fiery, gin-based cocktail, which burns bright in her honor. Careful not to get any egg white in your eye!

Trixie Mattel

Barbie's Gone Coconuts

Makes 4 drinks
- 1 cup (240 ml) light rum
- 2 cups (400 g) ice
- 1 (12 fl. oz./355 ml) can pink concentrated frozen lemonade
- ½ cup (120 ml) sweetened cream of coconut (such as Coco López)
- ¼ cup (60 ml) maraschino cherry juice (from jar)
- 4 tbsp whipped cream
Garnish: coconut flakes and maraschino cherries

Add all ingredients except whipped cream to a blender and blend until smooth. Pour into a soda fountain (milkshake) glass, top with whipped cream, and garnish. Serve with a straw. Invite over your very best Barbies, and enjoy.

Trixie Mattel's schedule is a lot like her makeup—all over the place! At any given moment, she might be promoting a *New York Times* bestselling book, retrofitting a Palm Springs motel, or working with frequent collaborator Katya Zamolodchikova on their latest web series or world tour. At this point, the fact that she won the third season of *All Stars* is practically an afterthought. Born Brian Michael Firkus, this queen rather iconically chose his first name as something of a fuck-you to his homophobic stepfather— who called him "a Trixie" anytime he acted effeminate. Trixie's last name and overall look stem from a less traumatic source: his deep (if somewhat questionable) love of all things Barbie.

A life-size, mod-era Barbie doll and self-described "skinny legend," Trixie is quick with a quip. "I like my men like I like my coffee," she said during an episode of *All Stars* in 2018, "Incapable of loving me back." Like any good comedian, she also knows how to spin her suffering into spools of gold for the enjoyment of others. "I'm not gay because my dad touched me, I'm gay because I loved it," she said in her 2019 documentary *Moving Parts*, before deadpanning: "I'm kidding, I didn't have a dad."

Trixie had been writing songs since she was thirteen, but failed to gain much traction until she started performing in drag. "Being a white guy with a guitar was, as it turns out, not that special," she joked during an *NPR* interview. Being a white guy with an autoharp, a wig, and some solid one-liners, though, was apparently the secret sauce she needed—and her career took off. Today, a Trixie performance is truly unparalleled among the queendom. She breathlessly switches from lip sync to comedy routine, to plucking an assortment of stringed instruments while singing original music—and is the most successful recording artist to emerge from the *Drag Race* galaxy.

Just like Trixie, this spiked milkshake is sweet, pink, and full of cream. Channel your inner soda jerk and whip up a batch for your next Tupperware party.

Pabllo Vittar

Cachaça-la-Casa-Down Botas

- 2 shots cachaça
- 1 shot Lillet Blanc
- ½ shot fresh lime juice
- 3 shots dry grapefruit soda (such as San Pellegrino Pompelmo)
Garnish: grapefruit wedge and a sprig of mint

Add cachaça, Lillet Blanc, and lime juice to a shaker filled with ice. Shake, then strain into a Hurricane glass filled with ice. Top with grapefruit soda, stir, and garnish. *Saúdé!*

Pabllo Vittar is not just Brazil's definitive drag performer—she's also a bona fide pop star and the most followed queen in the *world* (with over 12 million Instagram followers, dwarfing even Mama Ru!). She has released four studio albums; the first, called *Vai Passar Mal*, reached the third spot on Brazil's iTunes chart during its debut week. "Todo Dia", a song from that record, was picked as the official tune of Brazilian Carnival in 2017.

This queen's ascendant star has made her a much sought-after collaborator. In 2020, Pabllo featured as a model in a Calvin Klein underwear campaign for Pride Month. In 2021, she worked with Lady Gaga on a version of "Fun Tonight," done in the traditional Brazilian *forró* style, for Gaga's *Dawn of Chromatica* remix album. And in 2022, Pabllo was named a co-host of the HBO Max drag competition *Queen Star Brasil*. That same year, she became the first queen to perform at Coachella.

Originally, Pabllo's last name was Knowles, after the famous Australian children's author Sheena Knowles (kidding! It's Beyoncé, obviously). Later, she adopted her current masculine-sounding name to ensure audiences knew she was a cisgender man performing in drag. "Pabllo Vittar is a boy, who is a girl, who has no gender, who is not afraid," she said in an interview. But when those high heels come on, you best be using the feminine pronoun to address this queen. "I won't stand in front of the mirror for two hours putting on makeup for someone to call me 'he,' right?" she said. "Call me 'she'! 'She' is beautiful, 'she' is a singer, 'she' is a drag queen! I like to be called in the feminine."

This cocktail created in Pabllo's honor includes a healthy dose of Brazil's national booze, cachaça. Enjoy a batch while watching her music videos, which feature beautiful shots of her home country, high camp, and a sizzling make-out scene with music producer Diplo. You'll be booking tickets for the next Pabllo concert before you can say "Cachaça-la-Casa-Down Botas."

Shangela Laquifa Wadley

When she was cast in the second season of *Drag Race* in 2010, Shangela Laquifa Wadley had been doing drag for mere *months*—and wowed the judges with her talents (or, not so much—the baby queen was famously cut in the first episode). But she is living proof that if Mama Ru sees something special in you, she'll keep you around until your star is ready to shine. The very next season, Ru invited Shangela back; she entered the workroom by jumping out of a massive Christmas present with her trademark, "Halleloo!"

By her *All Stars* season in 2018, Shangela's drag was so polished and creative—featuring looks like a red-spiked dress that inflated as she walked down the runway—that she was the clear frontrunner. During the season finale, however, she was controversially eliminated. But for her booming touring career, multiple television and movie appearances, and millions of social media followers, Shangela, tragically, was left with *nothing*. Hopefully she found comfort in her little-known follow-up projects, like her turns in *A Star Is Born* and *Broad City*. Or her critically acclaimed, Emmy-nominated HBO show *We're Here*. Or her history-making appearance as the first drag contestant on *Dancing with the Stars*. Poor thing!

Despite her many accolades and accomplishments, Shangela's greatest role is one she played every night for a decade straight—as Jenifer Lewis's roommate. Originally, Shangela worked as an assistant to the legendary actress and singer. As Lewis explained in an interview, when Shangela was cast on *Drag Race*, Lewis told the queen she was "too famous" to be her assistant, adding, "But you can move into the house." So Shangela lived in Jenifer's basement apartment while chasing her own dreams of stardom, and the two became close friends, even co-hosting a short-lived web series together.

The cocktail inspired by this queen contains cognac, a spirit that must age for at least two years before it's any good—kind of like Shangela's drag. Halleloo!

Halleloo!

- 1 shot cognac (or brandy)
- 1 shot sweet vermouth
- ¾ shot aged rum
- ¼ shot (1½ tsp) grenadine
- ¼ shot (1½ tsp) fresh lemon juice
- 2 dashes Angostura bitters
Garnish: lime twist

Add all ingredients to a shaker filled with ice. Shake, strain into a chilled coupe glass, and garnish. Channel your inner Shangela and throw in the face of a girl who could *never* have a sugar daddy.

The Boulet Brothers

Dragula's Blood

• 1 shot gin
• 1 shot Cynar
• 1 shot Campari
Rim: fake blood
Garnish: sprig of rosemary
  and a small piece of dry ice

Rim a Martini glass
with fake blood. Add all
ingredients to a shaker
filled with ice. Shake,
strain into the prepared
glass, and garnish. To
avoid poisoning yourself,
wait until the dry ice has
died a slow, painful death
before serving. Or don't?
And see what happens.
Muahahaha!

If *RuPaul's Drag Race* took place in the underworld, you'd
get something akin to the show hosted by these two
queens … but you'd still need to add more fake blood. Known
separately as Dracmorda and Swanthula, but together
as the Boulet Brothers, this duo turned their longtime
nightclub act—where audience members regularly ended
up covered in "blood, fish guts, and confetti"—into what
is widely considered to be the best alt-drag competition
out there.

The Boulet Brothers' Dragula, which premiered in 2016,
sets out to crown the "World's Next Drag Supermonster"
and features runway categories like Killer Clown, Trash
Queen Couture, and Hellraiser. Contestants are judged not
based on their "charisma, uniqueness, nerve, and talent" as
they are on RuPaul's show, but on their looks' "filth, horror,
and glamor." The brothers are the first to warn anyone
brave enough to appear on the show that the competition
"isn't safe." The bottom two contestants in each episode
undergo "extermination challenges" that force them to face
fears such as being buried alive, eating cow intestines, and
surviving an evening in a haunted house.

Dracmorda and Swanthula have been widely praised
for helping showcase an edgier, more grotesque side
of the drag world, and for incorporating an inclusive
spectrum of drag across gender and identity. As *Vice* once
wrote in a profile, this duo is "loud, weird, and pisses on
heteronormativity." The winner of the first season, Vander
Von Odd, said the show "screams out to the weirdos and
the outsiders of the world that they're seen and they're
valuable, and there's a family of freaks out here waiting
for them."

A true cocktail in honor of the Boulet Brothers should
probably include cyanide. But since suggesting a poisonous
recipe apparently has legal ramifications, this drink uses
Cynar instead.

Kiki DuRane

Singer-songwriter and actor Justin Vivian Bond got the idea for Kiki DuRane, the character they are best known for, while sick one evening prior to a performance in the 1980s. Rather than cancel, they developed an intricate backstory to accompany their raspier-than-usual voice: she would be a haggard, washed-up lounge singer so old she knows Jesus "in the biblical sense." There's nothing New Yorkers love more than watching a diva get progressively more intoxicated onstage, so Kiki—and her piano player, the equally bedraggled Herb, aka Kenny Mellman—quickly developed a cult following. In the early 1990s, they performed in small venues like P.S. 122 and the Tex-Mex restaurant Cowgirl Hall of Fame. But as news of the cabaret act spread, Kiki and Herb started selling out Broadway theaters and picking up Tony nominations.

During a Kiki and Herb show, you might hear a cover of Tom Jones's "Sex Bomb," Eminem's "Lose Yourself," or Kermit the Frog's "Rainbow Connection." The range of Kiki's repertoire, however, is nothing compared to her interpretation of these hits. At times, her chaotic, full-throated rendition of "Total Eclipse of the Heart" would be just as appropriate for a hardcore concert as a Broadway stage. Between songs, Kiki treats audiences to drunk, rambling monologues that waver between stand-up routines and social commentary. She might remark on the learning disabilities of her granddaughter, Opioid, for instance, or bemoan that "between the AIDS and the Alzheimer's, we haven't got a fan left over forty."

Justin has killed off Kiki many times over the decades. Her first funeral took place at Carnegie Hall in 2004 during the show *Kiki and Herb Will Die for You.* In the years since, Justin has launched a successful solo career, regularly performing to sold-out crowds at downtown NYC venues Joe's Pub and La MaMa. Fortunately, much like Kiki's early lover, Jesus, her lounge act with Herb is periodically resurrected (most often during the holidays, for their show *Do You Hear What We Hear?*).

Like the iconic performer, this champagne cocktail, a version of a Death in the Afternoon, is classy—too classy, in fact, so be sure to tone it down with the bitters.

Kiki Loves You

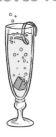

- 1 sugar cube
- 2 drops Peychaud's bitters
- 1 shot absinthe
- 4 shots chilled champagne
Garnish: lemon twist

Soak the sugar cube with bitters and drop into a champagne flute. Pour in absinthe, slowly top with chilled champagne, and garnish. Enjoy at Kiki's next funeral.

RuPaul

Sage Queen*

- 6 blackberries
- 2 sage leaves
- 2 shots fresh grapefruit juice
- 1 shot honey syrup (p. 15)
- 4 shots club soda (soda water)

Garnish: sage leaf and a blackberry

Add blackberries and sage leaves to a shaker and muddle. Fill the shaker with ice, then add grapefruit juice and honey syrup. Shake, then strain into a goblet-type glass with one large ice cube. Top with club soda, stir, and garnish with a sage leaf and a blackberry on a cocktail pick. Enjoy while feeling your "inner saboteur" melt away.

* This is a zero-proof cocktail.

How to describe the impact of this queen? Let's just say, thanks to RuPaul Charles, teenage girls in Wichita, Kansas, now routinely utter things like, "I'm gagged, slay, *okurrrr*?"

However, RuPaul's success was never a given. Before winning the first of many Emmys, she was earning her drag bona fides—like every other queen of her era—in dimly lit bars coated with questionable fluids. But she had her eyes trained on superstardom. Her first foray into the mainstream came in 1993 with the release of "Supermodel (You Better Work)." Its chart-topping success led to a modeling deal with MAC Cosmetics, a talk show co-hosted with her lifelong best friend (and future *Drag Race* judge) Michelle Visage, and more. By the end of the 1990s, a RuPaul cameo was *the* stamp of approval for any project trying for a camp sensibility, like *But I'm a Cheerleader* and *The Brady Bunch Movie*.

Indeed, Ru would stop at nothing short of a New World Order with drag squarely at its center. When she first started hosting *Drag Race* in 2009, the show was so low-budget it looked like it had been filmed through a thick layer of Vaseline. But thanks to the charisma, uniqueness, nerve, and talent of Ru and her queens, it developed a big following (and a bigger budget). With franchises now spanning the globe, and spin-offs that have put everyone from random housewives to Vanessa Williams in drag, Ru has yet to find the outer reaches of the *Drag Race* cosmos—and hopefully never will.

That said, not everyone is pleased with the mainstreaming of drag. Once an LGBTQ art form, today drag belongs to everyone—and no one. Yet RuPaul is too busy inspiring, mentoring, and launching the careers of a new generation of queens to pay haters any mind. But if you're craving the drag of yesteryear, head to your local queer bar: thanks to Ru, there are more drag artists performing in sticky back rooms than ever before.

For having the foresight to know the heights to which drag could ascend, toast RuPaul—our high lordess, savior, and sage queen—with this zero-proof cocktail created in her honor.

Sister Roma

Patriotic Pop

- 1 shot grenadine
- 2 shots lemon-flavored malt beverage (such as Mike's Hard Lemonade or Smirnoff Ice)
- 2 shots vodka (divided)
- ½ shot blue curaçao

Garnish: red, white, and blue popsicle (ice lolly)

Add grenadine to a highball glass and add crushed ice until about three-quarters full. In a separate glass, mix together the malt beverage and 1 shot of vodka. Pour mixture very slowly over the back of a spoon into the highball glass to create a second layer. In another glass, mix the remaining shot of vodka with blue curaçao, and again slowly pour over a spoon to create the final layer. To apply popsicle garnish, simply do as Sister Roma might say to one of her porn actors: just stick it in.

Sister Roma is a longtime member of the Sisters of Perpetual Indulgence, a hallowed order of clown-faced, bearded nuns based in San Francisco. The group combine the holy trinity of drag, high camp, and direct-action protests in their act to mock gender and religion—all while raising thousands of dollars for LGBTQ and HIV/AIDS causes.

Sister Roma first took her vows in 1987 and is today among the order's most prolific members and money-raisers. A self-proclaimed "loudmouth," she's a sought-after host at queer events, emceeing pride festivities across the world. Each year in San Francisco's Dolores Park she hosts a "Hunky Jesus" contest. Muscle-bound men dressed in togas and thorny crowns enter into righteous competition for the chance to be chosen as the one true and most yoked son of God—all in the name of raising awareness and funds for the queer community, of course.

However, it's not all prayers and rosaries for this queen; Sister Roma is among the LGBTQ community's fiercest advocates. In 1989 she started the Stop the Violence campaign to combat hate crimes in the San Francisco area. And in 2017 she launched an effort to pressure Facebook to drop the company's "real name" policy, which prevented many trans and nonbinary users of the platform from identifying by their chosen moniker.

When Sister Roma isn't raising money (and hell) in her nun's habit, she's serving the queer community in other critically important ways—such as by creating and directing gay pornography. For years, she worked as an artistic director for Hot House Entertainment and NakedSword, and co-hosted an online talk show to dissect the cinematic nuances of the industry's latest movies.

Created to rejoice in Sister Roma's steadfast service to our community and country, this cocktail is as patriotic as they come. Since there's no easy way to turn a failed healthcare system into a garnish, this beverage calls for the next most American thing out there: a tri-striped popsicle.

Jujubee

Good JuJudy*

- 1 pear, quartered, core removed
- 10 dried jujube dates, sliced lengthwise into threes
- ¼ cup (40 g) sliced fresh ginger
- 2 cinnamon sticks
- 1-2 tsp honey (to taste)
Garnish: pine nuts

Add 6 cups (1,440 ml) water, pear pieces, jujubes, ginger, and cinnamon sticks to a medium-sized pan and slowly bring to a boil. Reduce heat, cover, and simmer for 1 hour. Remove from heat and pour liquid through a strainer into a teapot. Pour into the finest teacup you have, stir in honey to taste, garnish with 6 to 8 pine nuts, and serve.

* This is a zero-proof cocktail.

There is perhaps no other soul, besides RuPaul herself, who is more synonymous with the *Drag Race* universe than this beloved queen. Starting in 2010, the mononymous Jujubee competed on the second season of *Drag Race*, following that with the first and fifth seasons of *All Stars*, plus *Drag Race: UK vs the World*. Then, of course, there are her numerous appearances on *Drag Race* spin-offs and competitions, with shows like *RuPaul's Drag U*, *RuPaul's Secret Celebrity Drag Race*, and *AJ and the Queen*. If you've actually seen all these iterations, condragulations! You're keeping Jujubee booked and busy (and Mama Ru very well fed).

In addition to her robust *Drag Race* schedule, Jujubee is also the host of the dating podcast *Queen of Hearts*, which connects singles looking for love using nothing more than their voices. She no doubt landed the gig thanks to her performance on an early episode of *All Stars*, during which she demonstrated her familiarity with the dating show format. "I'm Jujubee," she said during a random confessional moment, "I like long walks on the beach, big dicks, and fried chicken."

Though she has competed in more *Drag Race* franchises than any other queen—reaching the finale not once or twice, but *four* separate times—Jujubee has still never won the ultimate prize. However, she has snatched the aortas straight out of the chests of each and every one of her adoring fans.

Feeling violently sick with rage that your favorite queen has yet to come out on top? This hot tea remedy created in jubilation of Jujubee is just what the doctor ordered. A ginger-soaked elixir steeped with cinnamon and dried jujubes (naturally), it may not give this queen the crown she so rightly deserves, but it will hopefully provide some temporary relief while the world patiently waits for Ru to finally give her her flowers.

BenDeLaCreme

Is it possible for a drag queen to be, of all things, *nice*? For fans of this iconic performer, the answer is a resounding "You betcha!" BenDeLaCreme ("DeLa for short, De for shorter, Ms. Creme if you're nasty") has managed to prove the impossible: that drag can center positivity and good vibes without skimping on entertainment value. The DeLa brand is "terminally delightful," she says; "So positive she could cause death at any moment."

DeLa's drag is equal parts naughty pinup girl and mid-century housewife—the love child of Bettie Page and Lucy Ricardo. She shot to fame in 2014 on the sixth season of *Drag Race*, placing fifth overall but winning the Miss Congeniality vote from fans. DeLa returned to television for the third season of *All Stars*, where she became the first queen in *Drag Race* herstory to win five episode challenges in a single season. Widely considered the favorite to win the whole shebang, DeLa famously bowed out of the show mid-season. In interviews following her exit, which is today the stuff of lore, she explained she was simply no longer interested in the "bloodlust" created as a result of drag competitions.

DeLa may be kind, but don't let that fool you—she's quick with a joke. A DeLa performance is funny, but rarely at the expense of anyone else. Instead, she's serving Jennifer Coolidge character actress *realness*. During a *Bachelor* parody challenge on her *All Stars* season in 2018, DeLa embodied a drunken cougar who shamelessly flashes the camera with her kitty-cat while stumbling out of a limo. "I'm here to land me a boy-man," she slurs, while shimmying her giant breastplates. She is also among an elite group of comedy queens to have won Snatch Game not once but *twice*, as Maggie Smith and the campy game show panelist Paul Lynde (celebrities that few other entertainers, drag queens or otherwise, could have made as funny).

I creme, you creme, we all scream for "DeLa to the Crem-a!" So whip up a batch of this cream-forward cocktail and raise your glass to this kind, hilarious queen.

All Things Nice

- 1 shot green crème de menthe
- 1 shot white crème de cacao
- 2 shots heavy (double or whipping) cream
Garnish: cocoa powder

Add all ingredients to a shaker filled with ice. Shake, strain into a chilled coupe glass, and garnish with a light sprinkling of cocoa powder.

Linda Simpson

Bingo!

- 1 shot vodka
- 1 shot apricot brandy
- 1 shot triple sec (Cointreau)
- ½ shot fresh lemon juice
- ½ shot club soda (soda water)

Garnish: lemon wheel and a maraschino cherry

Add vodka, apricot brandy, triple sec, and lemon juice to a shaker filled with ice. Shake, then strain into an ice-filled Collins glass. Top with club soda, stir, and garnish with a lemon wheel and a maraschino cherry on a cocktail pick—and that's *bingo!*

This smarty-pants queen—who has reigned supreme over New York's East Village drag scene since the late 1980s—describes her onstage persona as a "flirty career girl." However, Linda Simpson is just as ambitious when the wig comes off. In 1987 she founded *My Comrade*, a magazine featuring photos and stories of the city's drag culture, go-go boys, and other nightlife shenanigans. In interviews, Linda said she wanted the mag to celebrate the queer joy she saw around her, even amid the AIDS epidemic and rampant LGBTQ oppression. Her covers ranged from the political ("Long Live the Gay Nation") to the playful ("Tits and Cocks Extravaganza") and featured many of her downtown sisters.

Throughout this time, Linda carried a point-and-shoot camera in her purse and captured thousands of photos of her fellow queens during nightly performances at venues like the Pyramid Club. In doing so, she documented the early days of queens like RuPaul and Lady Bunny when they were mere drag princesses. As drag entered the mainstream, Linda realized she had inadvertently chronicled the beginnings of an unstoppable cultural juggernaut. So, in 2012, she compiled her photos into an acclaimed slide show, *The Drag Explosion*, which later became a book. *Paper* magazine deemed her the "Thinking Woman's Drag Queen," while the *New York Times* conferred on her the honorary title of "Accidental Drag Historian."

Though she has performed the world over, appeared in movies and on television, and authored multiple books, her most impressive accomplishment is without a doubt this one: Linda Simpson is New York's preeminent bingo hostess. For years she has emceed game nights at any venue that will have her—bars, restaurants, and the Nordstrom on 57th Street.

Need to liven up your bingo night? Whip up a batch of this take on the classic Bingo cocktail, created in tribute to Linda. After a couple of these bad girls, your guests will surely be wielding their ink blotters with the enthusiasm of a thousand Floridian retirees.

Conchita Wurst

Spicy Phoenix

Makes 4 to 5 drinks
- 5 cardamom pods
- 4 cinnamon sticks
- 3 cloves
- 1 (25 fl. oz./750 ml) bottle dry red wine
- 1 orange, sliced
- 2–4 tbsp sugar (to taste)

Garnish: orange slices and cinnamon sticks (leftover from preparation)

Crush the cardamom pods on a cutting board using the back of a knife. Add the crushed cardamom, cinnamon sticks, and cloves to a large pot and dry-roast over medium-low heat for 5 minutes, stirring constantly to prevent burning. Add the wine, orange slices, and sugar to the pot. Stir carefully until liquid is hot, but not boiling. Reduce heat to low, then simmer for 30 minutes. Ladle into glass mugs with handles. Use orange slices and cinnamon from the pot as garnish. Grow a beard. Enjoy.

These days, a bearded queen is about as remarkable in the drag world as a death drop. But when Conchita Wurst first darkened drag's doorstep with her five-o'clock shadow—as a competitor on the 2014 Eurovision Song Contest, representing Austria—it was a sight to behold. With her song "Rise Like a Phoenix," she joined the ranks of legends like ABBA and Celine Dion by winning the whole damn thing—all while sporting a gold evening gown and full black beard. "The beard is a statement to say that you can achieve anything," she said in an interview. "No matter who you are or how you look."

Conchita's win helped shine a big ol' hairy spotlight on the vast and glorious world of genderfluid drag—which even *Drag Race* had largely avoided showcasing previously. The rise of Conchita, however, ensured scruffy queens would be clipped from culture no longer. RuPaul herself paid homage to the trend with a bearded runway challenge on the seventh season of *Drag Race* (Violet Chachki won, looking like the love child of Sleeping Beauty and a Bee Gees brother with her golden whiskers and pink Dior gown). Several *Drag Race* franchises have since included bearded queens in their casts, among them Danny Beard, who won the fourth season of the show's UK version.

Following her Eurovision triumph, Conchita toured the world, released several albums, and served as a judge on *Queen of Drags*, a German TV drag competition, alongside Heidi Klum. In recent years she's adopted even more androgyny into her aesthetic and has suggested she may one day leave the bearded look behind her completely. "I have achieved everything I wanted to," said Tom Neuwirth, the performer behind Conchita, in an interview. "I don't need her anymore. I have to kill her."

Dead or alive, Conchita has permanently changed the world of drag for the better. She's not the first to perform with facial hair, but, thanks to the visibility she brought to unkempt queens everywhere, she won't be the last, either. So heat up some wine, throw in some spices, and let your tastebuds rise like a phoenix in her honor.

Peaches Christ

Sex on the Peach

- 1 shot peach schnapps
- 2 shots fresh orange juice
- 1 shot vodka
- 2 shots cranberry juice
- ½ shot grenadine

Garnish: orange wedge and maraschino cherries

Add the peach schnapps and orange juice to a shaker filled with ice. Shake, then strain into a Hurricane glass filled with ice. Slowly pour in the vodka to create a second layer. In a separate glass, mix the cranberry juice and grenadine, then carefully pour over the back of a spoon into the drink for a beautiful, bloody ombré effect. Garnish with an orange wedge and maraschino cherries on a cocktail pick.

Peaches Christ first developed her alter ego while attending film school at Penn State University. For her senior thesis, she wrote and directed a family-friendly movie, *Jizzmopper: A Love Story*, which followed the travails of a janitor working at an adult video store. After casting herself as the female shopkeeper—the "matriarch of an enchanted wonderland" —she donned drag for the first time. Peaches Christ was thusly risen, and she has been delighting her devoted disciples ever since.

While continuing to write and direct shorts and movies (most notably 2010's *All About Evil*, a campy, murderous romp starring Natasha Lyonne, Mink Stole, and Cassandra Peterson, aka Elvira, Mistress of the Dark), Peaches began developing a cult following as a drag performer and hostess. For years, she appeared onstage at a San Francisco-based drag club, known today as Mother, that featured guest stars like Lady Gaga and Gwen Stefani. During Easter weekend, the queens would take the show on the road, driving a bus filled with extravagantly dressed and excessively intoxicated fans to Reno, Nevada, where a special performance, followed by brunch, awaited them.

For over a decade, Peaches hosted Midnight Mass, a horror movie screening series, at the Bridge Theater in San Francisco. As well as films, the evenings were packed with drag shows and costume contests—and sometimes featured guest ghouls like John Waters or Linda Blair. Though she hung up her hostess cape in 2019 to focus on other things, Peaches has since debuted a podcast by the same name. During each episode, she dissects her favorite films, horror or otherwise, alongside fellow filmmaker Michael Varrati. Devotees are known, appropriately enough, as "Children of the Pod-corn."

The cocktail inspired by this queen is very peach forward, of course. But this take on a Sex on the Beach comes with an extra shake or two of blood-red grenadine, in celebration of her love for horror.

Tayce

Tingly Crangarita

- 1½ shots mezcal
- 1 shot triple sec (Cointreau)
- 1 shot cranberry juice
- ½ shot fresh lime juice
- Splash of club soda (soda water)

Rim: lime wedge, 1 tbsp sugar mixed with 1 tbsp coarse (flaky) salt

Garnish: fresh cranberries

Rim a rocks glass by lining with a lime wedge and then dipping into the sugar and salt mixture. Add all ingredients except club soda to a shaker filled with ice. Shake, then strain into the prepared rocks glass filled with ice. Top with a splash of club soda and garnish with 3 or 4 fresh cranberries on a cocktail pick. Take a sip to wash down your antibiotics.

Well before Tayce was cast on the second season of *RuPaul's Drag Race UK*, where she placed as a runner-up, a McDonald's that she frequented in South Wales served as her original main stage. "I would wear a braided headband wig with a pink feather boa around my nipples," she once told British *Vogue*. This queen has been bending gender for so long, it never even dawned on her to develop a different name for her drag alter ego. "Beyoncé is Beyoncé," she said. "I've got a good name, so I'll keep it."

During her *Drag Race UK* season in 2021, Tayce's sisters bestowed on her the title of Trade Minister, for her dashing good looks when out of drag—and it appears the fashion world agrees. After the show, Tayce signed a contract with Models 1, Europe's biggest modeling agency. Today, she routinely struts down the catwalks of major fashion shows—both in and out of drag—and has appeared in campaigns for brands like Jean Paul Gaultier and Coca-Cola, and as a muse for makeup artist Pat McGrath.

In a candid moment while on *Drag Race UK*, Tayce discussed her history with chlamydia and gonorrhea, revealing to her fellow competitors that she had spent years wrestling with feelings of guilt and shame after contracting the infections when she was eighteen years old. Though it's no secret that drag queens *love* a good STI joke (Bianca Del Rio once quipped that her favorite things about Australia are "koalas and chlamydia"), Tayce's on-air admission represented a rare moment of openness about these incredibly common infections and was widely praised for helping shine a light on the subject.

This cocktail also celebrates Tayce's bravery in discussing a needlessly taboo topic, and includes a healthy dose of bacteria-fighting cranberry juice for good measure. (*Disclaimer: this cocktail will not cure your chlamydia.*)

Sherry Vine

Sherry Vine, born Keith Levy, is a veteran of New York's 1990s downtown drag scene. She is perhaps best known for her family-friendly live shows, which feature children's songs like "I Love Being a Whore!," "I Want to Suck You Now," and "Shit My Pants." (Depending on how much of a cool parent you are, you could actually let your kid listen to that last one.)

Human excrement has remained a surprisingly dominant—and troubling—motif throughout Sherry's oeuvre. In what many consider to be her finest work in this area, she reprised Natalia Imbruglia's "Torn," complete with the following inspired lyrics: "When did I eat corn? / I'm a bit confused / This is really strange / I'm scared, yes it's true / What the hell is in my poo?"

A longtime lover of the variety show format, Sherry was inspired to create her own in 2021: *The Sherry Vine Variety Show* on OutTV, a campy reimagining of the classic television genre (think a drunken *Donny and Marie* with lots of fart jokes). Sherry co-hosts alongside her bosom buddies Jackie Beat and Mario Diaz; segments include bizarro comedy sketches and musical numbers, plus an ensemble of guest stars like Bianca Del Rio, Alaska Thunderfuck 5000, and Candis Cayne. (The astute fan will remember that, once upon a time, Sherry actually hosted a similar drag variety show on Hulu, called *She's Living for This!*) Since 2014, Sherry has also starred in *The Golden Girlz*, a spoof of the beloved sitcom, at the Cavern Club Theater in Los Angeles. Given some of her naughty musical ditties, you won't be shocked to learn that she plays Blanche Devereaux.

A classy queen deserves an equally classy cocktail, which is why Sherry inspired this refreshing beverage, the When Did I Eat Corn? It's a take on the classic Bee's Knees, which dates back to the 1920s—right around the time this ancient queen was first getting her start.

When Did I Eat Corn?

- 2 tbsp fresh corn kernels
- ½ shot honey syrup (p. 15)
- ½ shot fresh lemon juice
- 2 shots gin

Garnish: corn wheel (2–3 kernels wide)

Add the corn kernels, honey syrup, and lemon juice to a shaker and muddle. Fill the shaker with ice and add gin. Shake, strain into a chilled coupe glass, and garnish. Enjoy— and try to remember: *this* is when you ate corn.

Raven

Ice Queen

- 1 shot vodka
- 1 shot rum
- 1 shot blue curaçao
- 1 shot Chambord
- ½ shot fresh lime juice
Garnish: sprig of mint,
  maraschino cherries,
  and blackberries

Add all ingredients to
a shaker filled with ice.
Shake, then strain into a
stemless wine glass filled
with crushed ice. Garnish
with mint, maraschino
cherries, and blackberries
on a cocktail pick. Enjoy
while critiquing your
friends' outfits.

Raven is arguably the most prolific queen within the *Drag Race* franchise, despite never having snatched a crown. She first wedged herself deep into our collective consciousness in 2010 as a competitor on the second season of *Drag Race*, following that up with the first season of *All Stars* in 2012. She's since left her contestant days far behind her, graduating to "professor" on *RuPaul's Drag U*, which aired for three seasons—and today is creative producer for both *Drag Race* and *All Stars*. A businesswoman!

Raven is also a gifted makeup artist and personally beats RuPaul's face senseless for each *Drag Race* appearance. Her work on the show even won her an Emmy in 2020 for Outstanding Contemporary Makeup for a Variety, Nonfiction or Reality Program.

In 2022, RuPaul gave a nod to Raven's powerful presence within *Drag Race* during the *All Winners* season of *All Stars*. After gathering the illustrious group of previous champions into the workroom on the first episode, Mama Ru duped them into thinking Raven would be competing as well—despite never having won. This is one queen, Ru seemed to imply, who needs no crown to reign supreme.

When Raven is *not* helping the entire *Drag Race* franchise continue its terrifying pace toward total world domination, she's critiquing it. In 2014, she and fellow *Drag Race* alum Raja started a YouTube series called *Drag Race Fashion Photo RuView*. The pair are known for their funny, if at times brutally honest, reviews of contestants' outfits—assigning a "toot" (good) or "boot" (bad) to each look. "Looks like a nice set she got at Bed, Bath & Beyond," Raven said of one queen's outfit. "Because of *that* boot, I give *this* a 'boot,'" she said in another episode.

Just like Raven, this blue-tinged cocktail created in her image is stunning, if a bit intimidating (is it even safe to drink blue things?). But that's exactly how this mysterious, dark ice queen likes it.

Alaska Thunderfuck 5000

Your Cocktail Is Terrible

For the meringue
- 3 egg whites
- ¼ tsp cream of tartar
- ¼ cup (50 g) granulated sugar

Using an electric mixer, beat egg whites in a bowl until frothy. Add cream of tartar and sugar, and beat until stiff peaks form.

For the cocktail
- 2 shots vanilla vodka
- ½ shot Chambord
- ½ shot pomegranate juice
- 1 scoop vanilla ice cream
- 2 shots meringue

Add vanilla vodka, Chambord, and pomegranate juice to a shaker filled with ice. Shake, then strain into a rocks glass. Drop in vanilla ice cream. Top with meringue and torch it with a hand-held kitchen torch until caramelized. Serve with a spoon.

At this point, it's *Drag Race* canon: thou shalt have an album drop immediately after appearing on the show—regardless of thine vocal abilities. Alaska Thunderfuck 5000 is no exception, but her discography is unique in one crucial respect: you've almost definitely heard her songs. Since her time on the show—which included a runner-up performance on season five of *Drag Race* in 2013 and a first-place showing in *All Stars* season two in 2016—she has released several Billboard-charting studio albums, including *Anus*, *Poundcake*, and *Vagina*. Some of her most celebrated songs are classics like "Hieeee," titled after her now infamous catchphrase, and inspirational anthems such as "Your Makeup Is Terrible."

Alaska has also come to dominate another media space chockablock with *Drag Race* queens: the podcast universe. (If you're a Ru Girl and you don't have your own podcast yet, do you even really drag?) *Race Chaser*, the show she hosts alongside fellow *Drag Race* survivor Willam Belli, is a fan favorite. While discussing each and every episode of *Drag Race*, the two queens serve up "tea, truths, and tee-hee-hees," according to one reviewer.

Originally from Erie, Pennsylvania, Alaska got her start in drag at the Pittsburgh dive bar Blue Moon, performing on a stage held together by, as she once put it, "Scotch tape and chewing gum." She's served many legendary looks over the years, but perhaps none more beloved than the one created for Lil' Poundcake, her alter ego. Conceived during a *Drag Race* mini-challenge, this clown-cum-voodoo-doll is available for purchase on Alaska's website … but she'll haunt your dreams completely for free.

Alaska named herself after a popular strain of the club drug marijuana that is known for its "creeper" effect and for enhancing appetites—a perfect description for this creepy queen, who can't seem to keep her fans satiated. The cocktail created for her is a take on the Baked Alaska, which, appropriately enough, is also the name of a popular type of weed. Common side effects of this strain, by the way, include arousal and panic attacks. Read into that what you will.

Jackie Beat

Bitter Queen

- 1 shot rye whiskey
- 1 shot Fernet-Branca
- ½ shot ginger liqueur
  (Domaine de Canton)
- ½ shot beet juice
- ½ shot fresh lemon juice
- ½ shot agave syrup
Garnish: sprig of thyme

Add all ingredients to
a shaker filled with ice.
Shake, strain into a chilled
coupe glass, and garnish.
Enjoy during your next
therapy session.

Kent Fuher first unleashed his foul-mouthed alter ego, Jackie Beat, on unsuspecting audiences in Los Angeles in the late 1980s. ("Shut the fuck up!" she'll retort to those who say that makes her old, "Being young is not an accomplishment!") Since then, Jackie has been touring the world, dazzling people with her sophisticated comedic stylings—a carefully calibrated blend of sardonic wit and poop jokes, which she parlays into parodies of pop hits, like "Baby Got Front" and "I Kissed a Squirrel."

Jackie is perhaps most celebrated for her annual Christmas show, which *Time Out New York* once called "an oasis of bile in a season of sappy sentiment." Each year, she adds to her arsenal of carol parodies with hits like "It's Beginning to Look a Lot Like Syphilis" and "Santa's Baby." "Christmas is all about artifice and magic," she told the *New York Times*, continuing, "and then with a dash of darkness, you add alcohol."

A veteran of The Second City, Chicago's legendary improv troupe, Jackie has also taken her comedy chops to the small screen. On her television series *Dr. Jackie: Unlicensed Psychotherapist*, which began airing in 2022, she gives what some might call "advice" to a rotating cast of clients. Famous folks like Elvira, Mistress of the Dark, Alec Mapa, and Margaret Cho have all graced her chair, as well as a steady stream of *Drag Race* alums like Bianca Del Rio and Alaska Thunderfuck 5000. Jackie's longtime friend and frequent collaborator Sherry Vine plays her "slutty blond assistant."

The cocktail created to toast Jackie is beet-based, for obvious reasons. It's also bitter as hell, just like her—but maybe she has good reason to be. She once said in an interview that she registered the name *Drag Race* with the Writers Guild of America well before her sister Ru ever got around to it. "If you have two brain cells to rub together," a reality show about drag is "going to be called *Drag Race*," she said. Still, she's not upset about her well-known friend's success, since "it's a bitch being more talented than famous."

Julian Eltinge

According to vaudeville comedian W. C. Fields, women "went into ecstasy" over this early 1900s performer—while men "went into the smoking room." During the height of his career, Julian Eltinge (born William Julian Dalton in 1881) was one of the highest-paid film and stage actors in the USA and arguably the best-known drag artist of his time.

Julian first showed a proclivity for drag at the impressionable age of ten, when his teacher Mrs. Wyman caught him mimicking the girls in her dance class. Rather than punish him for it, the remarkably woke-for-her-time educator (who shall henceforth be known as the Michelle Visage of the era) instead encouraged young Julian to explore the craft of female impersonation.

He first took his talents to the stages of vaudeville, where he made a name for himself thanks to his ability to "pass" as a cisgender woman. As one contemporary reviewer put it, he looked "remarkably well in women's togs" and managed the voice and mannerisms of "some members of the sex." As a result, Julian often stunned audiences at the end of his act when he removed his wig in dramatic fashion, shattering the illusion.

As word of his performances spread, Julian left vaudeville for bigger stages on Broadway and then Hollywood, where he took on roles in musicals and movies written specifically for him. In 1910 he starred in what would become his most successful show, *The Fascinating Widow*. In an article for the *New York Times*, actress Ruth Gordon said Julian's performance contributed to the "gaiety of nations" thanks to his ability to play a widow "more fascinatingly than if fascinating real widows played them."

Another reviewer once called him the "merriest of widows," which in turn has given inspiration to this drink concocted in homage to his legacy. It may not look like much, but drinker, beware: a couple of these will no doubt make you merry. Just like Julian, this seemingly dainty beverage has something to hide (hint: it's a lot of booze).

Merry Widow

- 1 shot mezcal
- 1 shot yellow Chartreuse
- 1 shot Aperol
- 1 shot fresh lime juice

Add all ingredients to a shaker filled with ice. Shake, then strain into a coupe glass.

Lypsinka

With a name like Lypsinka, this queen sets expectations high—and easily surpasses them. She has reigned as the world's *true* lip sync assassin since the early 1980s. However, you won't catch her mouthing along to Whitney or Madonna, as her muse is a different type of diva: Hollywood starlets of the past. One minute she's calmly getting ready for her close-up; seconds later, she's screeching, "But ya are, Blanche! Ya are in that chair!" A Lyspinka show includes so many references to classic movies that even a *New York Times* critic admitted he struggled to identify them all.

Eventually, Lypsinka took her act Off-Broadway, with show titles that sound like drag versions of 1990s compilation albums, including *Now It Can Be Lip-Synched*, *Lypsinka!* and *I Could Go On Lip-Synching*. During her show *Lypsinka! The Boxed Set*, she spent the better part of ten minutes answering a series of increasingly unhinged phone calls in the voices of Elizabeth Taylor, Joan Crawford, and Elizabeth Montgomery. The effect was "a kaleidoscopic nervous breakdown," according to one review, illuminating just how much the "hysterical dame" defined Hollywood's portrayal of women at the time.

This talented performer has taken on many non-Lypsinka roles over the years as well. In 2004, John Epperson, the artist behind Lypsinka, appeared as the Wicked Stepmother in the New York City Opera's revival of *Cinderella* alongside the legendary Eartha Kitt. John is also a classically trained pianist and has worked as the accompanist for the American Ballet Theater since the 1980s. His expertise in music—and dramatic women—also landed him what may have been the most perfectly cast role ever, as the "jaded piano player" in 2010's *Black Swan*.

In honor of Lypsinka, whip up this Gibson—the cocktail that famously loosened Bette Davis's tongue in *All About Eve*, providing Lypsinka with endless material. But careful there, dear Gibson Girl. After a couple of these booze-forward drinks, you might need to fasten your seatbelt. It's going to be a bumpy night.

Bumpy Night

• 1¾ shots gin
• ½ shot dry vermouth
Garnish: cocktail onions

Add the gin and vermouth to a shaker filled with ice. Shake, strain into a chilled Martini glass, and garnish with 3 cocktail onions on a cocktail pick. Enjoy while mouthing along to your favorite Criterion Collection movie.

Aquaria

Aquarian Stardust

For the lychee syrup
• 1 (20 oz./565 g) can of lychees (peeled and pitted) in syrup

Add the lychees, with their syrup, to a blender. Blend until smooth, and strain. Discard the pulp and store syrup up to one week in an airtight container.

For the cocktail
• 1½ shots tequila
• ½ shot blue curaçao
• 1 shot lychee syrup
• ½ shot fresh lemon juice
• 1 tsp edible glitter

Add all ingredients, including glitter, to a shaker filled with ice. Shake, strain into a wine glass, and then swirl, baby, swirl, for a shimmering treat.

Aquaria has been performing in some of New York's most popular queer clubs since before she could legally drink this cocktail created in her honor. As a teenager, she got her start under the watchful eyelashes of famed nightlife promoter Susanne Bartsch. Appearing onstage at parties like Holy Mountain and Battle Hymn—alongside club kid legends like Amanda Lepore and Richie Rich—Aquaria got an early education in how to survive an industry known for swallowing up young performers stilettos first. In interviews, she has credited these veterans for helping instill in her a strong work ethic and sense of professionalism, attributes that have come to define this hardworking queen.

When she first appeared on the tenth season of *Drag Race* in 2018, Aquaria was dismissed by many as nothing more than a pretty face. But she held her own against the season's comedy queens, even beating them at Snatch Game by embodying a hilariously bewildered Melania Trump. Clips of her performance went viral, and her stans circulated a petition demanding *Saturday Night Live* cast Aquaria as the former first lady. While she wasn't asked to be on *SNL*, she *was* crowned the season's winner, becoming the youngest queen to win the title in the show's herstory.

To be clear, Aquaria *is* first and foremost a queen who is "turning looks, stunting pretty" (as she sang on an episode of *Drag Race*). Since signing with IMG Models, she has appeared in *Vogue Italia*, on the cover of *New York* magazine, and in campaigns for everyone from MAC Cosmetics to Moschino. In 2019, she became the first drag queen to attend the Met Gala (sitting at the same table as Anna Wintour, no less). For her look, she wore a black gown made of ribbon by John Galliano, punctuated with a front-facing ponytail.

Periodically, Aquaria will bequeath makeup tutorials to her millions of social media fans. You, too, can beat your face like an oil-slicked mermaid or pull off that coveted "1980s-inspired drugstore" look! She's no stranger to glitter in these glow-ups, which has in turn inspired this cocktail, the Aquarian Stardust.

Pangina Heals

Hot-and-Sour Tom Yum

- 4 sprigs cilantro (coriander)
- 3–4 slices ginger
- 2 tsp lime zest
- 3 slices red chili
- 1½ shots tequila
- 1 shot triple sec (Cointreau)
- 1 shot fresh lime juice
Rim: lime wedge, 1 tbsp sugar mixed with 1 tbsp coarse (flaky) salt
Garnish: cilantro sprigs and chili slices

Line the rim of a rocks glass with a lime wedge, then dip into the sugar and salt mixture. Add cilantro, ginger, lime zest, and red chili slices to a shaker and muddle. Fill with ice, add tequila, triple sec, and lime juice, and shake. Strain into prepared rocks glass filled with ice, and garnish.

This is one queen you do not want to waack off with. Pangina Heals, Thailand's preeminent drag artist, is well known for crushing the competition by incorporating "waacking" into her performances—a voguing-adjacent dance featuring arm twirls and dramatic poses. Pangina first learned to waack under the tutelage of New York-based dancer Princess Lockerooo. She then took the style back to Bangkok, and you best believe she had *all* the girls waacking soon after.

Pangina first rose to fame as a performer and host at Maggie Choo's, a popular drag venue in Bangkok. Today, by many accounts, she's the most globally recognized drag artist in all of Asia (she's often referred to as the RuPaul of the region). Like Ru, she has made it her mission to mentor up-and-coming talent in the area, giving a platform to many drag performers at her own Bangkok bar, House of Heals.

No stranger to a drag competition, Pangina took part in Thailand's first televised drag contest, *T-Battle*, in 2014. Due to a fractured foot, she had to use a wheelchair for five weeks of the show—but she *still* waacked her way to first place. This iconnery caught the eye of Mama Ru, who tapped her to host *Drag Race Thailand*. Later, in 2022, she was cast on *RuPaul's Drag Race: UK vs the World*. Though a frontrunner and fan favorite, a fellow contestant sent Pangina home early in the competition—to the great consternation of many. *Drag Race* super-stans still cite her elimination as among the most controversial in the show's herstory (even RuPaul said it was "gut-wrenching").

Fortunately, Pangina has found a brilliant way to exact her revenge against the drag community. During her talk show, *Tongue Thai'd with Pangina Heals*, she conducts insightful interviews with fellow *Drag Race* queens as they eat progressively spicier Thai food (it's like *Hot Ones*, but with stilettos and curry). This spicy queen has in turn inspired an equally hot drink: a cocktail version of a tom yum soup.

Shea Couleé

I Came to Slay (the Crème Brulée)

For the glass
• Caramel sauce

Chill a Martini glass in the freezer for 10 minutes. Drizzle caramel sauce around the inside of the glass, then return to the freezer while you make the cocktail.

For the cocktail
• 2 shots vodka
• 1 shot vanilla liqueur
• 1 shot heavy (double or whipping) cream

Add all ingredients to a shaker filled with ice. Shake, then strain into the prepared Martini glass.

There is perhaps no other queen powerful enough to merge together the world's two most unwieldy cinematic universes—*Drag Race* and Marvel Comics—than Shea Couleé. In 2023, she became Marvel's first drag superhero when she joined the cast of the Disney+ series *Ironheart*. Shea was the obvious choice for the role, since she helped inspire Marvel's first drag character, Shade—who gets so pissed off after losing a drag competition she gains mutant powers.

Like Shade, Shea also famously lost a drag competition (thanks to Sasha Velour's show-stealing rose petal reveal on season nine of *Drag Race*), only to return in the form of the unstoppable, superhuman winner of *All Stars* season five in 2020. No "best of drag" list can be published, legally speaking, without including at least one of Shea's looks from her *All Stars* season. She served "Nubian goddess realness" one episode, dressed in a skintight, Swarovski-bejeweled jumpsuit, and a neon Lisa Frank caterpillar character the very next. She even paid tribute to her former foe, Sasha, with a *Carrie*-themed look—swapping out the bucket of blood for one filled with rose petals.

Shea has parlayed her *Drag Race* success into many other ventures. As well as being one of the most accomplished musicians to emerge from the franchise, with lyrics like "You can suck a D-I-dick / Pop a Nyquil daily cause I'm just that sick," Shea is without question *the* supreme rapping drag superstar. Still, the greatest accomplishment of this queen—who has performed alongside Christina Aguilera and been dressed by fashionistas including Christopher John Rogers and Pierpaolo Piccioli of Valentino—is this: Naomi Campbell once said her runway walk was "perfection." The two divas even have each other's phone numbers. "I can die very happy, because Naomi Campbell called me her friend," she told *W* magazine.

As Shea might say, she is smoother than "motherfucking crème brulée." So whip up a batch of this sweet caramel treat and slay a couple glasses in her honor.

Sin Wai Kin

Canadian-born visual artist Sin Wai Kin, previously known as Victoria Sin, exploded onto London's art scene in the early 2010s with their impersonations of old Hollywood starlets. Soon, this morphed into a type of performance that exaggerated femininity to its most extreme form; their trademark look often included a massive pair of prosthetic boobs and an equally gigantic blond wig. (Wai Kin once said they like hairpieces that could eat "your wig for breakfast.")

By taking an unattainable, maximalist version of the female body to almost clown-like proportions, Wai Kin's performances held gender up as something to laugh at, not normalize. "It's not about trying to be a perfect representation of a gender," they said; it's about "blowing up gender and identity completely."

In more recent years, Wai Kin, who is nonbinary, has started embodying (and making fun of) the masculine end of the gender spectrum. For a 2021 multimedia project titled *It's Always You*, they developed four separate drag characters, casting each as part of an imaginary boy band. As they detailed in an interview, Wai Kin intended to show how members of groups like these are distilled down to a single characteristic—like "the sexy one" or "the smart one"—so that they can't exist on their own; together, however, they become something approximating a whole person. In a video that forms part of the piece, the boys each take turns performing lyrics that could be ripped directly from the brain of superproducer Max Martin: "It's always you / you're the one in me / you tell my different sides / my multiplicity." As the Tate explained in a write-up about Wai Kin after their nomination for the prestigious Turner Prize in 2022, they are a performer who shows the world that drag can be used "as a means of deconstructing and challenging misogyny and racism in and outside of the queer community."

This cocktail created in Wai Kin's honor is bubbly and sophisticated, much like their drag. Pour a glass of the colorful concoction and toast the brilliance of a true artist. Be sure to make a batch big enough to enjoy with each of your personalities.

The Multiplicity

• 1½ shots grenadine
• ¾ shot apple brandy
• 4 shots sparkling wine
Garnish: lemon twist

Pour grenadine and apple brandy into a champagne flute. Slowly top with sparkling wine, and garnish.

Yvie Oddly

This queen hails from the drag scene in Denver, Colorado, where she got her start performing at local queer bar Tracks. She chose her drag name, Yvie Oddly, to let the girls know that she'll always be "even odder" than anybody else in the room. Yvie made a mark on the city's scene thanks to her dark-but-fun aesthetic, turning it out with cheap materials from thrift stores. It was a skill born out of financial necessity, but one that ultimately impressed RuPaul: Yvie competed on, and won, the eleventh season of *Drag Race* in 2019.

Yvie may be a drag superstar, fashionista, and recording artist, but her biggest accomplishment is of course her massive penis. Her ding-dong became a running joke throughout her season of *All Stars* (as Jinkx Monsoon said, her dick is so big, "when she tucks, she has to tape it between her shoulder blades"). Yvie handled the attention like a gentlelady. "I think it speaks pretty well to my character," she said in an interview. "If all people really have to say about me is I have a big dick—my god! *That's* the worst part about me?"

Yvie lives with hypermobile Ehlers-Danlos syndrome, a connective tissue disorder that means she can contort her body into impressive shapes while she performs—but also means she lives with constant pain. Yvie has said that one of the best things to come from her time on *Drag Race* is the connection she has made to the broader world of people living with similar conditions. Her decision to speak publicly, she said, "opened me up to the fact that there are so many people struggling with this or with other invisible disabilities, and I never realized there was such a major community of people."

Yvie's tribute cocktail—which includes a pinch of turmeric to help with inflammation—is based on the super classy Boulevardier. So be sure to add a penis-shaped swizzle stick to dumb it down a bit (after all, Yvie's dick is *so* big, when tickets went on sale to see it, Ticketmaster crashed!).

Big Oddly Energy

- 2 shots Scotch
- 1 shot sweet vermouth
- 1 shot Campari
- 1 pinch ground turmeric
Garnish: orange twist

Add all ingredients to a shaker filled with ice. Shake, strain into a rocks glass filled with ice, garnish, and stir with a tasteful, penis-shaped swizzle stick.

Joey Arias

Joey Arias rose to fame not by looking like a famous pop diva but by sounding like one. Close your eyes during his covers of "All of Me" or "Them There Eyes," and for a moment you'll be transported to the Apollo Theater listening to Billie Holiday herself.

In the 1970s, before assuming his drag identity, Joey was a recording artist with Capitol Records, where he sang with the rock group Purlie. Later, he joined The Groundlings, the infamous comedy troupe that counts Will Ferrell, Kristen Wiig, and Maya Rudolph as alumni. Joey considers himself a singer first, and never really identified his act as "drag." But after honing his character, Joey found a welcoming home in New York City's downtown art and drag scenes. Among many other gigs, he emceed a legendary drag show at the since closed venue Bar d'O throughout the 1990s.

The rest of Joey's résumé reads like a top-ten list of iconic queer cultural moments. Google David Bowie's 1979 performance on *Saturday Night Live* and you'll see Joey singing backup, alongside the equally legendary performance artist (and Joey's good friend) Klaus Nomi. Rewatch the 1995 cult drag classic movie *To Wong Foo, Thanks for Everything! Julie Newmar*, and you'll see Joey kiki-ing beside fellow queens RuPaul, Lady Bunny, and Miss Coco Peru.

Later in his career, Joey left the background to perform center stage, where he belongs. In 2003, much to the consternation of his loyal NYC following, Cirque du Soleil hired the diva to star in and write songs for *Zumanity* in Las Vegas. After a six-year run, he returned to the Big Apple to star in *Arias with a Twist*, an Off-Broadway show he co-created with the puppeteer Basil Twist. Today, you can find this icon regularly selling out downtown performance spaces like Joe's Pub.

Gardenias were famously Billie Holiday's favorite behind-the-ear accoutrement, a detail that Joey regularly incorporates into his own look. To properly toast this star of stage, screen, and the back rooms of New York City dive bars, serve this cocktail on an overflowing bed of gardenias.

Billie's Holiday

- 6 fresh blackberries
- 1½ shots cognac (or brandy)
- ¾ shot triple sec (Cointreau)
- 1½ shots pineapple juice
- ½ shot fresh lemon juice

Garnish: orange twist and a gardenia for your hair

Add blackberries to a shaker and muddle. Fill shaker with ice and add the rest of the ingredients. Shake, strain into a Nick and Nora glass, and garnish.

Peppermint

Peppermint Crush

- 2 shots vanilla vodka
- 1 shot white crème de cacao
- 1 shot peppermint schnapps

Rim: marshmallow creme and crushed peppermint candy

Garnish: red gel icing

For the rim, spread marshmallow creme onto a small plate. Next, crush peppermint candy in a sealable plastic bag, then place it on a separate plate. Dip a chilled Martini glass first into the marshmallow creme and then into the crushed candy. For the cocktail, add all ingredients to a shaker filled with ice. Shake, strain into the prepared Martini glass, and garnish with a swirl of red gel icing on top of the drink.

Peppermint (or Miss Peppermint Gummybear in mixed company) shot to fame in 2017 on the ninth season of *Drag Race*, where she made history as the first contestant to enter the workroom as an out transgender woman. However, Peppermint had been dipping her patty into multiple forms of entertainment since well before her *Drag Race* days.

She first hit New York's nightlife scene in the 1990s, performing at legendary but long-shuttered venues like Tunnel. Later, she was tapped to appear as a drag version of Tyra Banks on *America's Next Top Model*, striking fear into the souls of that season's contestants ("You can't compete with a drag queen!" one correctly proclaimed). In 2016, she was featured in a *Daily Show* segment alongside other transgender rights advocates.

She did all this, and *then* decided to grace us with her standout performance on *Drag Race*, which has only launched her deeper into the stratosphere of drag stardom. Just months after her season aired, Peppermint announced she would become the first out trans woman to originate a lead role on Broadway. The show, *Head over Heels*, is loosely based on the sixteenth-century play *The Countess of Pembroke's Arcadia*—the plot updated ever so slightly to incorporate musical numbers set to songs by The Go-Go's. In 2018, Peppermint played an oracle in the show, giving a performance *Entertainment Weekly* called "ethereal and commanding."

That same year, Peppermint appeared in a sketch on *Saturday Night Live*, voicing the "drag entertainer" setting on a GPS system ("Turnt around, turnt around," she commands, after host Steve Carrell misses his exit). She's also released several albums, EPs, and singles, including *A Girl Like Me*, the first in a trilogy in which she opens up about her experiences as a Black trans woman, including her romantic entanglements with cisgender men.

No drink bearing Peppermint's name can forgo excessive amounts of sugar. Just like this trailblazer of a queen, the cocktail is so sweet it'll give you a toothache (seriously, you should brush your teeth afterwards).

Violet Chachki

Cinched Stem

- 2 shots gin
- ⅓ shot (2 tsp) crème de violette
- ⅓ shot (2 tsp) peach liqueur
- ½ shot fresh lemon juice
- 2 mint leaves

Garnish: edible purple pansy

Add all ingredients, including mint, to a shaker filled with ice. Shake, strain into a chilled coupe glass, and garnish.

This queen's last name is a variation on *tchotchke*, a Yiddish word commonly translating to "a small collectible item that gathers dust on the shelf of your spinster aunt's home." However, as it turns out, Violet Chachki's last name also means "beautiful young lady" in the same language. It's anyone's guess which definition the high-fashion star—who has worked as a lingerie model and walked New York Fashion Week—is nodding to with her glamorous persona.

From the moment Violet graced the *Drag Race* workroom in 2015, she became a fan favorite. Ultimately, she snatched the season seven crown thanks to her ability to turn looks that defy the very laws of physics. Known for cinching her waist to within an inch of her life (and lung capacity), she once stomped the runway accessorized with an oxygen mask and tank. She also gifted the world with one of the show's best "runway Ruveals," twirling out of a black sequined dress and into a red plaid jumpsuit like an elegant, bedazzled Transformer. Millions of *Drag Race* seasons from now, our dragcestors will no doubt still be referencing this pivotal moment in herstory.

Violet is also a darling of the burlesque world. She was among the performers picked to work on Dita Von Teese's 2017 revue *The Art of the Teese* and has since gone on to headline her own solo shows. Though she can do some damage with her aerial silks, her first love will forever be fashion. A frequent guest on runways around the world, Violet often steals the spotlight (and *Vogue* headlines—the magazine once called her the "Queen of Couture") with her own looks. Like everything she does, this is very much by design. "I want fashion and pop culture to see queer people as we are," she told *Vogue*, "Strong, beautiful, and confident."

The cocktail created in Violet's honor is strong as well, with three different types of booze. It's also, naturally, bursting with violet. Pour into a coupe glass with the most snatched stem you can find.

Panti Bliss

Not many queens can claim their very own political scandal, but Pandora "Panti" Bliss, Ireland's most famous drag performer, certainly can. During a 2014 appearance on a popular TV talk show on RTÉ, the country's national broadcaster, Panti called out two well-known journalists for being "really horrible and mean about gays." They sued for defamation, prompting RTÉ to issue them an apology—and an 85,000-euro settlement.

Pantigate, as the ensuing drama became known, roiled the country for weeks. Hundreds of journalists condemned the network's decision to apologize for Panti's statements, and the issue was even debated in the Irish parliament. Panti was finally invited to address the controversy at Ireland's National Theatre. Dressed in a stately purple gown, she told the mostly straight audience, "I don't hate you because you're homophobic—I admire you because most of you are just a *bit* homophobic." The speech went so viral that the Pet Shop Boys released a remix of it.

However, this queen has been advocating for the LGBTQ community since long before Pantigate. In 1995, the year Panti received a positive HIV diagnosis, she went on the radio to discuss her status publicly, to promote awareness. She was also front and center during the country's marriage equality battle. Same-sex marriage ultimately won legal recognition in Ireland in 2015; a documentary made the same year, *Queen of Ireland*, covers her critical role in the campaign's success.

Fortunately, Panti still finds time to perform—and not just at Pantibar, the queer pub she has owned since 2007 in Dublin. In 2023 she joined the Irish version of *Dancing with the Stars*, becoming the first queen to compete on the show. Though she mostly appeared in drag, she insisted on dancing at least once while dressed as a man. "I want there to be two boys dancing on TV," she said of the pasodoble she performed to "It's a Sin" (the feelings between Panti and the Pet Shop Boys are clearly mutual). "I think that's kind of important, to not have the faffery around it."

Obviously, there will be no "faffery" in a cocktail toasting Panti either. Whip up this take on an Irish classic, the Black Velvet, and raise your glass to a true class act.

The Pantigate

- 2 shots Guinness
- 2 shots champagne

Carefully pour Guinness into a large coupe glass. Then slowly pour in the champagne, letting it create a nice frothy head on top. Best enjoyed atop a soapbox.

Gottmik

Does a Body Good

- 1 shot cognac (or brandy)
- 1 shot dark rum
- 4 shots whole milk
- 1 tsp sugar
- 2 dashes vanilla extract
Garnish: fresh nutmeg

Add all ingredients to a shaker filled with ice. Stir, then strain into a large goblet filled with crushed ice. Grate some fresh nutmeg on top.

Beyond his ability to vocal fry words like "gorge" and "hot" until they're burnt and crispy, Gottmik may be best known as the first openly transgender man to compete on *Drag Race*, in 2021. His mark on the show, and on drag generally, however, goes far beyond this barrier-breaking milestone.

Dressed as the punk-rock harlequin clown of our dreams, Gottmik routinely crushed and subverted runway challenges onscreen like few before her. A "fascinator," for Gottmik, wasn't a tiny hat secured with clips but a giant, skull-piercing safety pin complete with a dangling, bedazzled blood droplet. Ask her to wear a "little black dress," and she'll comply—only with a doll-sized frock *so* little it barely covers her crotch.

If you're an A-list celebrity and Gottmik hasn't worked with you yet … you might have been demoted to the B-list, babes. A talented makeup artist, he has long beaten the faces of the rich and famous, including models from Cindy Crawford to Heidi Klum. His Rolodex includes pop stars too: in 2020, Lil Nas X tapped Gottmik to transform him into an eerily convincing Nicki Minaj for Halloween. A couple of years later, Sam Smith and Kim Petras recruited Gottmik (along with bestie and *No Gorge* podcast co-host Violet Chachki) to appear in the duo's chart-topping "Unholy" video and Grammy performance.

This history-making queen has helped redefine drag and continues to push the boundaries with her looks and makeup artistry. Gottmik perhaps summarized his own legacy best: "Gender is stupid," he said in an interview. "I want to tear it apart and play with it and confuse people."

This lactose-forward cocktail is an ode to Gottmik's name and trademark milky-white beat. Make a batch, say a toast to her, and then take a hearty sip—or better yet, chug it; Gottmik does a body good.

Gloria Groove

Groovy Caipirinha

- 3 strawberries, roughly chopped
- ½ lime, cut into 2 wedges
- 1 tsp agave syrup
- 2 sprigs mint
- 1 dash cinnamon
- 1 shot cachaça
Garnish: sprig of mint

Add all ingredients except cachaça to a shaker and muddle. Fill shaker with enough ice for one glass and add cachaça. Shake, pour into a small rocks glass, and garnish.

"I'm Gloria Groove from Brazil," this queen raps on her first single, "Dona," from 2016, "I've come to stay." These were prophetic lyrics, as it would turn out. The music video for the song—featuring a trippy kaleidoscope of fellow Brazilian dancers and drag artists—earned 1.7 million views in its first year (and has since been watched many millions of times more). Gloria followed that success with several studio albums, including *O Proceder* and *Lady Leste*, the latter of which reached the number-one spot on Spotify's Top Albums: Debut Global list in February 2022. Today, she is one of the most popular recording artists in all of Brazil, with songs that blend hip-hop, trap, and baile funk.

However, her music career is far from Gloria's first brush with stardom. Well before he became a drag diva sensation, Daniel Garcia Felicione Napoleão was singing with the popular children's musical group Turma do Balão Mágico ("The Magic Balloon Gang"). As a teenager, Daniel performed in theater, and he tried drag for the first time after taking on the role of Margaret Mead in the musical *Hair*. The experience inspired him to have a go at creating his own drag persona. Soon after, this groovy Brazilian pop sensation was born.

Today, Gloria's fanbase, which has global reach, has grown so large she is now the second most followed queen on social media—like, *in the world*—after fellow Brazilian drag popstar Pabllo Vittar. If the country's top two divas were cast in a Brazilian telenovela, they would be mortal enemies—or at least engaged in a hopeless love triangle. Instead, these *rainhas* are good friends and frequent collaborators who know how to put on a show. In the video for their song "Ameianoite," they make out and fight the patriarchy together by casting spells as lesbian witches.

In "Dona," Gloria calls for a "shout-out to all the drag queens of our nation." What better way to do so than with a batch of these strawberry caipirinhas made in her honor.

Elishaly D'witshes

When was the last time you were truly gagged at a drag show? Like so gagged, you choked on your vodka soda? If you've seen Elishaly D'witshes anytime recently, you'll have your answer. When she performs outdoors at Palace Bar in Miami's South Beach and a double-decker bus drives by, she'll sashay her way to the second story, hang off the side, lip sync a couple of bars, and then fall to the ground in the splits. For reasons that should be obvious, she is known by the moniker "Queen of the Bus." (Keanu Reeves found dead in a ditch!)

Videos of Elishaly's stunts have gone viral, garnering millions of views. She's done the bus gag so many times that the drivers in the area know her: "They honk their horns and open the doors to the bus so I can jump in," she said in an interview. But what if there's no bus nearby? Fear not, drag fan. Instead, this acrobatic queen might simply shimmy up the nearest pole and drop to the ground in the splits, before jumping back to her feet mid-*paso básico*. Or maybe she'll do a dizzying number of cartwheels during a lip sync while two helpful assistants throw buckets of water on her. No matter where you see her, she will be serving you *stunts*.

Shockingly, Elishaly has never been injured doing any of her tricks. She performs them so often, she's said, that she barely thinks about the charisma, uniqueness, nerve, and talent required to pull them off. However, when she watches her own viral videos, even she will admit it can be shocking to see some of her moves. "People tell me I'm crazy for doing that," she once quipped; "Sometimes I believe it myself."

Unless you're a gymnast, or Yvie Oddly, please do *not* try Elishaly's stunts at home. Let your taste buds do the somersaults instead with this rum-based shooter (based, appropriately enough, on a shot called 151 Ways to Die) concocted in her honor.

Stunt Queen

- ½ shot 151-proof (75% abv) rum
- ½ shot whiskey
- ½ shot tequila
- ½ shot high-proof grain alcohol (such as Everclear or Grain Neutral Spirit)
Chaser: lime wedge, Angostura bitters, and powdered (icing) sugar

To make the chaser, place lime wedge on a plate and soak in bitters, then dust with sugar. Add all cocktail ingredients to a shaker filled with ice. Shake, then strain into a double shot glass. Drink shot, bite into lime wedge, do the splits.

Valentina

Valentina's drag persona was inspired, in her words, by "strong, feminine Latina figures." She even cites one particular diva, Our Lady of Guadalupe—one of Mexico's national symbols—as her "drag mother."

This stunning queen is known for weaving smart, artful references to her heritage throughout her drag looks and performances. Some are easy to spot, like the oversized Mexican rose Valentina commonly wears in her hair. Others are sprinkled into shows like little *dulces escondidos*. In one of her most iconic looks on the *Drag Race* main stage during season nine, she wore a jeweled snake necklace and python-print dress. Everyone could appreciate the camp value—but fans of María Félix, the beloved Mexican actor and singer known for her serpent affinity, no doubt picked up on the deeper meaning.

Valentina is a performer who could go viral just by sneezing—which would be kind of perfect, actually, given her fondness for face coverings. Her first brush with internet immortality came in 2017 after RuPaul stopped a lip-sync-for-your-life smackdown, for the first time in *Drag Race* herstory, to ask Valentina to remove the bejeweled mask covering her mouth. Valentina's iconic response to Ru, "I'd like to keep it on, please"—because she didn't know the words to Ariana Grande's "Greedy"—has since been emblazoned across T-shirts, mugs, and even tattoos. The phrase also became something of an unofficial rallying cry for commonsense mask-wearers during Covid-19 lockdowns.

Valentina is the type of queen who gets attention even when *other* people talk about her. When fellow season nine competitor Aja LaBeija complained about Valentina's status as a judges' darling, the clip went viral—inadvertently pushing her rival even further into the spotlight. Music producer Adam Joseph went on to remix Aja's shady comments ("You're perfect, you're beautiful, you look like Linda Evangelista!") into a club song that can still be heard at queer parties the world over.

This spicy queen chose her drag name after the most popular hot sauce in all of Mexico. So while the brand of light beer called for in this cocktail is negotiable, the *salsa picante* better be Valentina.

Your Smile Is Beautiful

- 2 shots mango juice or nectar
- 1 shot fresh lime juice
- 1-2 dashes hot sauce (ideally Valentina brand)
- ½ bottle (approx. 5½ fl. oz./170 ml) Mexican light beer

Rim: lime wedge and Tajín
Garnish: fresh mango

Line the rim of a rocks glass with a lime wedge, then dip in Tajín. Fill the prepared glass halfway with crushed ice, add all ingredients except beer, and stir. Top with beer and garnish with mango chunks on a cocktail pick.

Eureka O'Hara

If you've ever seen Eureka O'Hara perform, you'll know the experience comes with a superhuman number of spins, dips, and kicks. Unfortunately, during season nine of *Drag Race* in 2017, she became the first contestant in the show's history to be eliminated for health reasons, after her knee popped during a cheerleading challenge.

Fortunately, Eureka came back the next season—and proved that no queen can pull off a jumpsuit fantasy like she can (and that *includes* Harry Styles). Her skintight, feathered entrance getup had her looking like a glamorous rooster that had fled the coop to become a Vegas showgirl. Later that season she served the judges a CEO villainess—complete with caped, body-hugging houndstooth suit—ready to fire her entire upper management team. Whatever fantasy Eureka gives, she does it with curves (and pads) in all the right places. "Proprortionizing!" as this glamazon might say.

With a personality and heart to match, she was an obvious casting choice for the Emmy-nominated HBO reality show *We're Here*, which follows queens as they travel through drag-starved areas of the USA. Apart from serving even more incredible looks, Eureka uses the platform to advocate for self-love and LGBTQ rights. After working with two trans people on the show, a young girl and an older woman who transitioned at the age of seventy, Eureka was inspired to come out herself. "I'm a trans woman," she said; "It just clicked."

Eureka, who stands at 6 feet 4 inches out of heels, is also a fierce advocate for body positivity. "Start expressing yourself," the self-appointed "elephant queen" said in an interview when asked what advice she'd give to other plus-sized people. "Wear the clothes you want without fear." Her music conveys similar themes, with inspiring lyrics like "Big-boned and sexy thick girl / Still catching dick, girl / Watch me spin, dip, and kick, girl."

To toast Eureka—who brings it to you every ball, risking life and literal limb in the process—create a batch of this popping candy-rimmed fruit punch. Let your tongue pop in her honor, rather than your knee.

Knee Pops*

- 2 shots coconut-flavored sparkling water
- 1 shot non-alcoholic blue curaçao
- ¼ shot (1½ tsp) pineapple juice
- ¼ shot (1½ tsp) cranberry juice

Rim: lime wedge and 1 packet tropical-flavor popping candy

Line the rim of a rocks glass with a lime wedge and then dip into the popping candy. Add all ingredients to a shaker filled with ice. Shake, then strain into the prepared rocks glass filled with ice. Sip and let your tongue spin, dip, and kick, girl!

* This is a zero-proof cocktail.

Paolo Ballesteros

Paolo Ballesteros is arguably the best-known drag performer based in the Philippines, a country with no shortage of talent. In 2001, at just nineteen years old, he got his start in the public eye as a host on the long-running show *Eat Bulaga!*, which features musical acts, comedy sketches, and a lot of entertaining randomness. In one segment, Paolo kept his eyes open for an hour and seventeen minutes without blinking, setting a world record in the process.

He is known as the king of makeup transformation, and with good reason: armed with little more than a brush, he can turn himself into pretty much anyone. Beyoncé, Rihanna, Meryl Streep, and almost the entire *Game of Thrones* cast have all received the Paolo treatment. Honestly, if you're a celebrity and he *hasn't* lionized you with one of his glow-ups by now, what are you even doing with your life?

Paolo also stars in movies, which heavily feature his makeup abilities as well—along with some amazingly Bizarro World plots. In *Die Beautiful*, he plays a character whose last wish is to be presented as a different female celebrity each day of her wake. In *The Panti Sisters*, he portrays one of three gay brothers who must each produce a grandchild for their rich but dying father, or forgo their inheritance.

When RuPaul announced the launch of *Drag Race Philippines* in 2022, she tapped Paolo to host the show—good thing, too, since there would surely have been riots in the streets otherwise. The series celebrates many of the queens from the country's booming scene, but it's still Paolo's looks—most of which showcase the work of local Filipino designers like Ehrran Montoya, Mara Chua, and Carl Arcusa—that have people talking the next day.

The cocktail created in Paolo's honor is, naturally, gin-forward, since Filipinos consume more of the juniper berry spirit than any other country! Be sure to use purple gin (infused with butterfly pea blossom) to toast this shape-shifting queen properly. A couple of shots of this stuff and your drink will transform before your very eyes.

The Transformer

- 2 shots club soda (soda water)
- 1½ shots fresh grapefruit juice
- 1 shot simple syrup (p. 15)
- ½ shot fresh lemon juice
- 2 shots gin infused with butterfly pea flowers (Empress 1908 or Lythan Positively Purple)

Garnish: grapefruit slices and a sprig of thyme

Add all ingredients except gin to a stemless wine glass full of ice, and stir. Top with gin, drop in 2 grapefruit slices, garnish with thyme, and stir to see the purple change to pink!

Willow Pill

Electric Bathtub

- 1½ shots dark rum
- 1½ shots light rum
- 1½ shots pineapple juice
- 1 shot sweetened cream of coconut (such as Coco López)
- ¾ shot fresh orange juice

Garnish: sprig of mint and toasted nutmeg

First, prepare the toasted nutmeg by adding 1 whole nutmeg to a pan and toasting over medium heat for 3 to 5 minutes, stirring constantly to prevent burning. Remove to a plate and set aside to cool. Add all the cocktail ingredients to a shaker filled with ice. Shake, then strain into a Hurricane glass filled with crushed ice. Garnish with mint and a fresh grating of the toasted nutmeg. Serve with a straw and enjoy during your next bath (toaster optional).

Nobody describes Willow Pill better than herself: as her website puts it, she's an "adorable, fun, and twisted little doll" from "your sweetest dreams and grossest nightmares." Her aesthetic is among the most unique ever to grace *Drag Race*; she somehow manages to be poignant, funny, *and* dark within the same performance. During one main stage appearance, Willow dumped a glass of red wine, a plate of spaghetti, and a toaster into a bathtub—while wearing a floor-length nightgown and lip syncing to Enya's "Only Time."

Willow has been open about her experiences living with cystinosis, a rare and chronic illness that causes widespread tissue and organ damage. Among her symptoms is constant exhaustion, but you wouldn't know it from her breakout performance on the fourteenth season of *Drag Race* in 2022. "When you are someone who's been dealing with chronic illness or a disability, you find your way to make it through the world and through daily life," she told *People* magazine when asked how she mustered the energy to not just slay, but snatch the crown, while filming the grueling reality show.

Thanks to her oddball humor and earnestness about her personal struggles, Willow quickly became a fan favorite during her time on the small screen. But this is one queen who knows how to keep people on their toes. Eager to push back on her status as a *Drag Race* darling, she lip synced to an original song, titled "I Hate People," during her season finale. Still, her misanthropic performance to the Deee-Lite-inspired house track—which involved the reveals of several additional Willow heads—likely had the opposite effect. Not long after her win, the *New York Times* included her on a list of the "most stylish people" of the year.

Willow's condition requires her to take upwards of twenty pills every day—a reality she recognizes and makes light of with her drag name. The cocktail created to toast her, a take on the classic Painkiller, is an attempt to do the same.

Raja Gemini

Raja Gemini was among the first *Drag Race* contestants to show that kooky queens can be glamorous—and winners too, baby. She snatched the crown during the show's third season, in 2011, thanks to her campy, high-fashion looks. Raja is the kind of performer who keeps fans of drag on their toes (most of whom *still* won't see eye to eye with her: she stands at 6 feet 3 inches out of heels). One moment she's serving Purple People Eater with an eyeball hat and the next a futuristic sexbot known as She-3PO.

In 2022, RuPaul invited Raja back to *Drag Race* to compete on an *All Winners* season of *All Stars*, providing an opportunity for an entire new generation of fans to fall in love with her. Most memorably, Raja—who often incorporates her Indonesian background into her drag—performed a traditional Balinese dance called the *kebyar duduk*, in the process creating one of the most high-profile examples of queer Indonesian culture ever to appear on television. And while Raja didn't win, Ru bestowed on her an accolade arguably just as prestigious: Queen of She Done Already Done Had Herses, for winning the season's Lip Sync LaLaPaRuza Smackdown.

Most YouTube channels these days are hosted by either a conspiracy theorist or a former *Drag Race* contestant—but amid the plethora of drag-themed shows, Raja hosts the standout *Drag Race Fashion Photo RuView* alongside her sister Raven. Raja, who holds a "master's degree in fierce," generously uses her pedigree on each episode to school the drag delusional. Together, the queens "toot" (that's good, for the heteros reading) or "boot" (that's bad!) literally every look to sashay down the runway. Raja's critiques range from the devastatingly brutal ("I think she looks like shit") to nuanced shade ("It looks like she's wearing really expensive paper towels"). More often than not, you'll find yourself agreeing with her.

Any drink honoring Raja needs to be elegant, original, and just a tad bitter. So shake up a batch of this refreshing white wine-based spritz and raise a toast to this stunning queen.

Toot Bootin' Sauv Blanc

- 3 shots Sauvignon blanc
- ½ shot Aperol
- ½ shot fresh lemon juice
- ½ shot dry grapefruit soda (such as San Pellegrino Pompelmo)
- ¼ shot club soda (soda water)

Garnish: orange wedge

Add Sauvignon blanc, Aperol, and lemon juice to a shaker filled with ice. Shake, then strain into a wine glass filled with ice. Top with grapefruit soda and club soda, stir, and garnish. It's a toot!

Landon Cider

Slip 'n' Cider**

- 1 cup (240 ml) apple cider (cloudy apple juice)
- ½ shot fresh lemon juice
- 1 ginger tea bag
- 2 dashes Angostura bitters
Garnish: lemon wheel and a cinnamon stick

Add apple cider and lemon juice to a saucepan and bring to a simmer. Turn off the heat, add the tea bag, and steep for 3 to 5 minutes. Pour the hot tea into a glass mug, add the bitters, and garnish.

** This is a low-proof cocktail.

Born Kristine Bellaluna, drag king Landon Cider describes his aesthetic as "glamdrogynous storytelling" and uses his looks to explore, honor, and dissect masculinity in all its forms. "Sometimes I'm super masculine," he said in an interview, "Sometimes I'm a soft, feminine man who just wants to get fucked in the butt, you know?"

Though he has long been a well-known entity in drag venues across California, Landon rose to broader fame after competing on *The Boulet Brothers' Dragula*. In 2019, he became season three's Drag Supermonster, as well as the first drag king to win any reality show competition in the United States—like, *ever*.

Landon ate spiders and jumped out of an airplane during his season of *Dragula*, so few would doubt he deserved the title. But it was his dazzling-yet-demented looks, many with a political edge, that ultimately spooked the judges into bestowing on him the win. During a "Vampire Burlesque" challenge, the queer Mexican American king dressed as a zombie mariachi player while holding a quart of "blood brew" emblazoned with the label "fuck your wall." This being a burlesque challenge, he naturally stripped down to his unmentionables while sensually pouring blood all over himself.

Although Landon is one of the best-known drag kings performing today, he's on a quest to ensure he won't be the last. "Kings can reign just as supreme as queens," he said in an interview. Though kings have long been relegated to the shadows cast by "big dick energy," he continued, "now we can buy our big dicks so easily on Amazon."

In 2022, Landon took his mission to another drag competition, Canadian reality show *Call Me Mother*, where he serves as a mentor for up-and-coming kings and non-binary performers—who are finally starting to enter the mainstream, thanks in large part to trailblazers like him. Toast this iconic king with a cocktail whose base—you guessed it!—is cider.

Alyssa Edwards

Bourbon Tongue Pop

- 2 shots bourbon
- 1 shot Ancho Reyes Chile Liqueur
- ½ shot fresh lemon juice
- 2 orange wedges
Rim: orange wedge, 1 tbsp sugar mixed with ½ tsp ancho chile powder

Bitch, line half the rim of a rocks glass with an orange wedge and then dip it into the sugar-chile mixture, girl. Add the bourbon, chile liqueur, and lemon juice to the prepared glass with one large ice cube, and stir. Gently squeeze the juice from the other orange wedges and drop into the drink. Sit yo' bitch ass down and enjoy, *bitch*.

This queen first rose to fame thanks to what she can do with her mouth. While Alyssa Edwards may not have invented the iconic tongue pop (that distinction goes to the creators of language), she *is* widely credited with helping bring it to the masses—having popped her tongue (and run her mouth) through the entirety of the fifth season of *Drag Race* and the second season of *All Stars*.

She got her start doing drag in Texas, choosing her name as an ode to Alyssa Milano, the actress known best for her role on *Who's the Boss?* and for looking stern in the back rows of US congressional hearings. Well before her *Drag Race* days, Alyssa was a prolific pageant queen, competing in and winning contests across the country (that'll be *Miss Shining Star Continental 2009* to *you*, honey!). On *Drag Race* in 2013, she quickly became a fan favorite thanks to the high pageantry she served on the main stage—and the high drama she brought to the workroom. A typical Alyssa quote starts and ends with the word "girl" or "bitch," with drag word salad in the middle. ("Bitch, sit yo' ass down and shut the hell up, bitch!" is but one example of her artful phrasing.)

Behind her sharp, popped tongue, however, is a kind and giving queen. Founder of the Haus of Edwards, Alyssa has birthed an impressively large brood of drag babies, many of whom have followed in her stilettos to become *Drag Race* stars in their own right. (She counts Shangela, Laganja Estranja, Gia Gunn, and Plastique Tiara among her progeny.) A trained dancer and choreographer, Alyssa's natural mothering instincts are also on display in Netflix's 2018 documentary series *Dancing Queen*, a surprisingly heartwarming look into her dance studio in Mesquite, Texas.

Alyssa's particular brand of Southern charm may be less "bless your heart" than it is "watch your back (rolls)," but her unfiltered mouth has made her one of the most beloved queens to emerge from the *Drag Race* empire. Everyone's favorite spitfire inspired this equally spicy cocktail—packed with just enough jalapeño to force your tongue to pop, and burn, in her honor.

Vanessa Vanjie Mateo

Vanessa Vanjie Mateo, better known simply as Miss Vanjie, may have been the first to be eliminated from season ten of *Drag Race* in 2018, but this is one queen who knows how to turn ten minutes of fame into an eternity. After slowly backing off the main stage while defiantly repeating her own name, she went viral. Even heterosexuals get in on the fun! Everyone from Andrew Garfield to Kathy Griffin has mimicked her infamous exit. Vanjie rode this single moment to gain millions of followers and a global touring career, writing a new *Drag Race* rule in the process: every eliminated queen now attempts a last gasp at stardom by coming up with an iconic exit line. But let's just say that, as of this writing, Andrew Garfield has yet to repeat anyone else's.

RuPaul was so tickled by Vanjie's elimination that she brought her back the next season (when she made it to fifth place). Ru then had her return as a "lip sync assassin" on *All Stars*. Then again for *RuPaul's Drag Race: Vegas Revue*. And then *again* as a guest judge on *Canada's Drag Race*. Vanjie offers her fellow queens an important life lesson: make RuPaul laugh, and you are family for life (Ru once even wore a "Vanjie" necklace to the Time100 Gala).

Vanjie is among the most naturally funny queens to have graced the *Drag Race* main stage, often needing to do little more than open her mouth: a thirty-minute YouTube compilation of her saying "Get these cookies, baby" has been viewed tens of thousands of times. Like her drag mother, Alexis Mateo—who bequeathed to Vanjie her drag name, thanks to the Puerto Rican flourish she infuses into the word "banjee"—she also has her fair share of fun with the English language. "Like a hooker on Rodeo Drive, she's kinda ghetto," she said of her aesthetic in a *Drag Race* confessional. "But, you know, still *eloquents*."

If you give a queen a cookie, she's going to ask for a cocktail—which is why this Oreo-garnished drink was created in honor of the truly one-of-a-kind Miss Vanjie.

Get These Cookies

- 1½ shots vanilla vodka
- 1½ shots dark crème de cacao
- ¾ shot heavy (double or whipping) cream
Garnish: crushed Oreos

Add all ingredients to a shaker filled with ice. Shake, strain into a chilled Martini glass, and garnish with these cookies, baby!

The Vivienne

This queen had her drag name picked out well before she even thought about donning her first blond bombshell wig. As a teenager, James Lee Williams earned the nickname "Vivienne" thanks to a reputation for strutting down the streets of Liverpool wearing head-to-toe Vivienne Westwood. Once she started performing, she adopted the nickname professionally. "I didn't want one of those cheap, nasty, slutty drag names," she said in an interview, "So I thought of 'The Vivienne' and here she is—there's only one of them."

However, don't be fooled by all the couture: The Vivienne has got jokes. After Donald Trump began his reign of terror in 2016, every comedian was forced to debase themselves with an impersonation of him. But The Viv gave Alec Baldwin and Jimmy Fallon a run for their money with her particularly creepy (and orange) take on the former president while competing on the first season of *RuPaul's Drag Race UK* in 2019. ("A bath of piss, that's how I keep my color," she said at one point.) She not only won her season's Snatch Game episode but reprised the role, alongside fellow UK queen Baga Chipz's Margaret Thatcher, in a six-episode parody web series called *Morning T&T*.

The Vivienne ended up winning *Drag Race UK*—and hasn't left our television screens since. Besides competing in the *All Winners* season of *All Stars* in 2022 (and being the only non-American queen to do so), she also hosted her very own reality show, *The Vivienne Takes on Hollywood*, on BBC Three, which documented her journey to make a music video in La La Land. And, even though Vivienne Westwood never got around to designing ice skates, The Vivienne also agreed to become the first drag queen to compete on *Dancing on Ice*, where she made fast enemies with the show's wardrobe department. "I come in on the day before the show and I say: 'Can we put like another ten thousand rhinestones on that please?'" she quipped in an interview.

The Vivienne's cocktail is a nod to a slightly lesser-known British royal, Queen Elizabeth, whose favorite drink was a Gin and Dubonnet.

Fit for a Queen

- 2 shots Dubonnet
- 1 shot gin

Garnish: lemon twist

Add ingredients to a shaker filled with ice. Shake, strain into a chilled Nick and Nora glass, and garnish. Bedazzle glass with ten thousand rhinestones (optional).

Adore Delano

The Party

- 1 tomatillo, quartered
- 2 jalapeño slices
  (seeds removed)
- 2 sprigs cilantro (coriander)
- ½ lime, cut into 4 wedges
- 1 pinch sugar
- 1 shot mezcal
- ½ shot triple sec
  (Cointreau)
Rim: lime wedge, 1 tbsp
  sugar mixed with 1 tbsp
  coarse (flaky) salt
Garnish: cilantro sprig and
  a lime wedge

Line the rim of a rocks glass
with a lime wedge, then
dip into the sugar and salt
mixture. Add tomatillo,
jalapeño, cilantro, lime
wedges, and sugar to a
shaker and muddle. Add
mezcal and triple sec and
fill with ice. Shake, strain
into prepared rocks glass
filled with ice, and garnish.

This queen reportedly picked her last name, "Delano,"
because it means "of the night" in Old French. As it turns
out, it also means "of the anus" in Spanish—read into that
what you like.

Adore Delano competed on the sixth season of *Drag Race*
in 2014, placing in the top three alongside Courtney Act
and winner Bianca Del Rio, whom she now counts among
her closest bosom buddies. Adore can glam it up with the
best of the divas when she wants to, but this punk rocker
is better known for her ability to throw on an oversized
Nirvana shirt with some ripped fishnets—and look flawless.

In 2016 she returned to the small screen for the second
season of *All Stars* but infamously bowed out early,
becoming the first *Drag Race* contestant in herstory to
do so. Though her decision was controversial, she simply
realized she didn't want or need the extra face time with
fans. She was already one of the most famous drag queens
on the planet—and today counts over 2 million followers on
Instagram.

Even before *Drag Race*, Adore was no stranger to reality
shows. In 2008 she competed (out of drag) on the seventh
season of *American Idol* (under her given name, Daniel
Noriega), making it to the semi-finals. She was cut early
after singing "Tainted Love" by Soft Cell—a performance
that Simon Cowell, the show's resident grouchy-pants,
called "grotesque." Daniel's sassy-aggressive response
("*Some* people weren't liking it," complete with a dramatic
neck swivel in Cowell's direction) earned her a viral social
media moment and a spot on Ellen DeGeneres's talk show
to discuss her controversial elimination. Later, Adore
revealed that *Idol* producers told her to "tone down" the gay
if she wanted to succeed—thank goddess she didn't listen.

In the words of this verbose queen: "Party!" This mezcal
cocktail will be sure to liven *yours* up. Don't "tone down" the
jalapeños—Adore likes things spicy.

Sasha Velour

At this point, *Drag Race* "reveals" are so expected they make M. Night Shyamalan blush. But in the finale of season nine, Sasha Velour managed to set a new standard. During the climax of Whitney Houston's "So Emotional," the bald-headed queen slowly removed her wig, causing red rose petals hidden underneath to cascade to the ground around her. The show-stealing lip sync earned her the season's crown, but the real honor came later: a parody on *Saturday Night Live* courtesy of Kate McKinnon.

However, this multitalented queen already boasted a fascinating résumé before *Drag Race*. In one previous life, Sasha wrote and sold successful comic books; in another, she studied contemporary Russian art on a Fulbright scholarship. Since *Drag Race* in 2017, she's focused on turning her rose petals into a full-blown bouquet of beautiful genderqueer artistry. Her production company, House of Velour (which *Fast Company* once proclaimed was "disrupting the business of drag"), produces projects that push the form's boundaries. Sasha's one-woman show, *Smoke & Mirrors*, incorporated stunning visual art, elevating drag beyond a "sickening lip sync or a fierce lewk," according to *Paper* magazine. And her long-running Brooklyn-based drag revue, *NightGowns*, which showcases a diverse range of artists, has become so popular it's spawned a Roku docuseries. In 2023 she released a book, *The Big Reveal: An Illustrated Manifesto of Drag*—which is of course the second most important book ever written on the subject.

As the worlds of drag and fashion have collided, Sasha has been at the center of the pileup. In 2018 she teamed up with Opening Ceremony to host a runway show featuring all LGBTQ models, while for Markarian's Fall 2023 collection Sasha slinked down the catwalk in a show-stopping red sequined gown. Whether serving looks from the front row or the runway, Sasha has said it "makes a lot of sense" to incorporate more drag into fashion. In both industries, "it's all about the clothes and what kind of stories we tell."

The cocktail created to toast this true artist is inspired by what she's best known for: contemporary Russian art. Kidding! A drink in Sasha's honor naturally needs to incorporate as many roses as possible.

Rim Around the Rosie

- 1½ shots gin
- ½–1 shot rose water (to taste)
- ½ shot fresh lemon juice
- ½ shot simple syrup (p. 15)
- 1 shot chilled sparkling wine
Rim: lemon wedge, 1 tbsp sugar mixed with 1 tbsp finely chopped dried rose petals
Garnish: dried rose petals and a lemon wheel

Rim a coupe glass by lining with a lemon wedge, then dipping into the sugar and rose petal mixture. Add the gin, rose water, lemon juice, and simple syrup to a cocktail shaker filled with ice. Shake, then strain into the prepared glass, top with sparkling wine, and garnish.

Symone

Symone has graced the cover of *Interview* magazine, walked Rihanna's Savage X Fenty show, and made Anna Wintour's invite list for the Met Gala. But the very first place this glamazon appeared in drag is unquestionably the most iconic: Olive Garden. After practicing her makeup skills in secret throughout high school, Symone debuted her drag persona publicly at the restaurant on the night of her prom. Despite the Italian eatery's promises, she was *not* treated like family that evening. "Some people got up and left but I stood my ground," she said in an interview.

Fortunately, she found a more supportive atmosphere later in life in the form of a drag troupe, House of Avalon. The crew have collaborated with everyone from Moschino to Cash App but are best known for the glamorous chaos they inflict on Los Angeles clubs. One night you might catch members in coordinated Care Bear outfits, and the next wrestling in a butter-filled kiddie pool.

In 2021, Symone won season thirteen of *Drag Race*, where she impressed with her creative and poignant looks. During one challenge, she sported a long, baby-blue durag that trailed behind her as she walked to celebrate the stigmatized headpiece as a "beautiful, Black part of our culture." For another outfit, she wore a white gown emblazoned with red Swarovski crystals in the shape of bullet holes and the phrase "Say Their Names" on the back. Her voiceover, played atop the footage of her runway walk, did just that: "Breonna Taylor, George Floyd, Brayla Stone, Trayvon Martin, Tony McDade, Nina Pop, Monika Diamond."

The *New York Times* wrote that Symone's drag is a "love letter to Blackness and queerness," but Rihanna put it more succinctly: "You soooo EVERYTHING! Nasty lil bitch! I live for every second of it!" she DMed the queen. It was a particularly meaningful tribute, Symone said, since RiRi is one of the Black female icons (along with Lil' Kim, Grace Jones, and Whitney Houston) who inspire her femme-fatale looks.

Just like Symone gives body-ody-ody, this crisp cocktail serves boozy-oozy-oozy, with three types of liquor. In the words of this wise queen: don't let the smooth taste fool ya, baby!

The "Nasty Lil Bitch!"

- ¾ shot Amaro Nonino
- ¾ shot Aperol
- ¾ shot bourbon
- ¾ shot fresh lemon juice
Garnish: lemon twist

Add all ingredients to a shaker filled with ice. Shake, strain into a chilled coupe glass, and garnish.

About the Authors and Illustrator

David Dodge (aka Hisperma S. Potent) is a freelance writer living in New York City who covers travel, LGBTQ stuff, politics, and culture. As well as being a frequent contributor to the *New York Times*, his work has appeared in outlets including *Travel + Leisure*, *CN Traveler*, *Out*, *The Advocate*, *Newsweek*, and more. He is the co-author of *Sassy Planet* (2021), *NYC Storefronts* (2022), and *Brooklyn Storefronts* (forthcoming, 2024), all published by Prestel. He is a huge fan of craft cocktail making and drag, but his own previous attempts at both have been described by friends as "not drinkable" and "upsetting," respectively. Still, he is thrilled to debut his new drag alter ego, Hisperma S. Potent—a name that no one but he seems to find funny.

David Orton (aka Brunhilde) is a freelance graphic designer whose client list includes Jim Beam, Nissan, and Estée Lauder. He lives in New York City with his husband, Nikolai Samsonov, and their extensive collection of candles. He is responsible for the cocktail recipes included in this book. Though he is not a professional bartender, and has never been paid to lip sync, he has nonetheless spent decades perfecting both art forms in the privacy of his West Village apartment for the forced enjoyment of his friends. After the second round of drinks, his alter ego, Brunhilde, often emerges: a Swedish dominatrix who fled Weimar Berlin in 1933 and now resides in Marrakesh, where she volunteers at an exotic bird sanctuary. Her interests include chunky jewelry, train travel, and her enormous wealth, the source of which is a mystery. Brunhilde has no known last name.

Cheyne Gallarde is a queer artist and illustrator born and raised in Hawaii but now living in Los Angeles. His illustrations combine LGBTQ icons and pop culture with comic book superheroes and villains. He has worked for clients including Netflix, Adobe, True Religion, Mattel, Family Equality, Logo TV, and Johnson & Johnson. In 2023, he provided illustrations for the book *Hispanic Star: Sylvia Rivera*, about the transgender rights activist, and in 2020 he illustrated the cover of the book *Legendary Children: The First Decade of RuPaul's Drag Race and the Last Century of Queer Life.* When not illustrating, Cheyne loves to decorate his *Animal Crossing* island, binge-watch reality TV and horror movies, and chill with his rescue dog, Rocket.

Acknowledgments

David Dodge and David Orton: First and foremost, we need to thank our editor, Ali Gitlow, for helping make this project happen—and for working with us to create a serious cocktail book that doesn't take itself *too* seriously (this is *drag*, for Peaches Christ's sake!). We are also so thankful for the opportunity to work with Cheyne Gallarde, who drew all of the stunning images in the book. Like asking Bob Ross to paint some happy little trees, there was truly no one better suited to the job. Thanks as well to Aimee Selby for copyediting and editorial support, and to Tom Joyes for designing the book. We'd also like to thank our many friends who are drag enthusiasts for their incredible suggestions. We apologize to those same friends for not being able to include most of them.

Content warning: earnestness! We have to take a moment to thank all the artists who appear in this book, as well as every drag performer who has ever lived in the entire country, globe, and galaxy, for not only entertaining us but being our community's fiercest advocates. At every point in our fight for equality and acceptance, kings and queens have been leading the way. This includes William Dorsey Swann, who was routinely arrested for hosting drag balls in the 1880s in Washington, DC. In fighting back, he became among the first people ever to advocate publicly for freedom of gender expression and identity. It also includes the many drag and trans performers and activists who helped spark the 1969 Stonewall uprisings and the modern-day LGBTQ rights movement. And, of course, it also includes the kings and queens of today— who keep performing despite the persistent best efforts of some ridiculously harebrained politicians and their supporters to ban the art form. Whoever's dumb idea it was to turn drag performers into political pawns has no idea what they're in for—a stiletto heel can quickly turn into a weapon of mass destruction.

As Bob the Drag Queen once said, drag is like armor. It makes sense, then, that queens and kings are always at the front lines of the fight for equality. A heartfelt thank you to these warriors.

© Prestel Verlag, Munich · London · New York, 2024
A member of Penguin Random House Verlagsgruppe GmbH
Neumarkter Strasse 28 · 81673 Munich

© for the text by David Dodge and David Orton, 2024
© for the illustrations by Cheyne Gallarde, 2024

Library of Congress Control Number: 2023942964

A CIP catalogue record for this book
is available from the British Library.

Editorial direction: Ali Gitlow
Copyediting and proofreading: Aimee Selby
Design and layout: Tom Joyes
Production management: Luisa Klose
Separations: Schnieber Graphik, Munich
Printing and binding: Livonia Print, Riga
Paper: Magno Natural

MIX
Paper | Supporting
responsible forestry
FSC® C002795
www.fsc.org

Penguin Random House Verlagsgruppe FSC® N001967

Printed in Latvia

ISBN 978-3-7913-8980-6
www.prestel.com